THE NEW MERMAIDS

The Changeling

THE NEW MERMAIDS

General Editors

PHILIP BROCKBANK

Professor of English, University of York

BRIAN MORRIS

Professor of English, University of Sheffield

The Changeling

THOMAS MIDDLETON
AND WILLIAM ROWLEY

Edited by PATRICIA THOMSON

ERNEST BENN LIMITED
LONDON

First published in this form 1964
by Ernest Benn Limited
25 New Street Square · Fleet Street · London · EC4A 3JA
Second (revised) Impression 1971
Third Impression 1974
© Ernest Benn Limited 1964
Distributed in Canada by
The General Publishing Company Limited, Toronto
Printed in Great Britain
Paperback ISBN 0 510–34106–3

CONTENTS

INTRODUCTION

THE AUTHORS

Much more is known of Middleton than of his collaborator, Rowley, whose life is very little documented. Thomas Middleton was born in London in 1580. His father, a man of some substance, a 'citizen and bricklayer', died when Thomas was only five years old and his school and university studies were clearly pursued against a turbulent, litigious background of suits raised by his mother against his adventurer stepfather. Although he matriculated at Queen's College, Oxford, in 1598, he probably did not take a degree.

In 1597 he published his first work, *The Wisdom of Solomon Paraphrased* (described by Swinburne as 'a tideless and interminable sea of fruitless and inexhaustible drivel') followed by other pamphlets in prose and verse. By 1600 he was settled in London 'daylie accompaninge the players', and by 1603 Middleton, now married, was writing comedies for Henslowe and others.

Throughout the first ten or fifteen years of the century Middleton wrote many successful comedies and intrigues of town life. Such plays as *Michaelmas Term*, *A Trick to Catch the Old One* and *A Mad World my Masters* carry the familiar Middleton apparatus of sharpers and usurers, tradesmen and courtesans, rich widows and gallants on the make—a seamy picture of London life which, while it has affinities with Jonson's, is without the latter's strong moral sense. Many of Middleton's characters are vicious and his irony heartless, but in these plays are some of the funniest scenes in Jacobean comedy—as, for instance, the christening scene in *A Chaste Maid in Cheapside*.

Around twenty-five plays have been definitely attributed to Middleton.[1] Collaboration with Webster, Dekker, Beaumont and Rowley helped to give variety to his output, e.g. *A Fair Quarrel*, in collaboration with Rowley, is a tragi-comedy of a very different outlook from his earlier plays, with its discussion of 'honour' and the ethics of duelling. There is, in fact, considerable variety in Middleton's output: comedies, tragi-comedies, pageants and masques for city occasions (he became City Chronologer in 1620), a political satire, *A Game at Chess*, which caused a furore and two great tragedies, *Women Beware Women* and *The Changeling*.

Nothing is known of William Rowley's early life although his dates are *c*. 1585–*c*. 1625. Information about him is derived from his stage-connections. He was a well-known actor with Prince Charles's men from 1609–*c*. 1612, specializing in playing comedy rôles— clowns, and comic villains—and in 1623 he was a prominent member of the King's Company and is known to have played the Fat Bishop in Middleton's *A Game at Chess*. He wrote four plays unaided but collaborated in at least eleven others with Middleton, Dekker, Day, Webster, Massinger among others. His own best-known play is a tragedy, *All's Lost by Lust* (*c*. 1619), which is full of heroic type-characters and noble sentiments, but is completely lacking in psychological motivation. His natural bent, both in acting and writing, seems to have been towards comedy and his *A New Wonder, A Woman Never Vext* is a pleasant

---

[1] Some critics—Oliphant, Barker and Schoenbaum, for example— have attributed *The Revenger's Tragedy* to Middleton.

well-handled citizen comedy which, in its good-humour, comes near to Dekker. His most successful collaboration was with Middleton, and it is clear that each stimulated qualities in the other not normally seen in their unaided work. Rowley probably collaborated with him in *A Fair Quarrel* (1615–16), *The World Tossed at Tennis* (1620), *The Old Law* (*c.* 1615), *The Spanish Gypsy* (1623), as well as in *The Changeling* (1622).

Critics are almost unanimously agreed, from the evidence of style and treatment, upon the allocation of the opening and closing scenes of the play and the sub-plot to Rowley, and the remainder to Middleton. In other words, Rowley introduces the characters and sets the play in motion, then concentrates his energies on the intrigue and fooling in the mad-house, till the last scene of Act V, while Middleton is responsible for the main action and the great Beatrice-Joanna, De Flores scenes. Verbal characteristics of V (ii) incline me to suspect that Rowley at least had a hand in that scene [it is one on which C. W. Stork, in his Introduction (1910) to *All's Lost by Lust*, expressed doubt] but, on the whole, the division of the play is unquestioned.

SOURCES

The main source of the play is the fourth story in Book I of John Reynolds' *The Triumphs of Gods Revenge against The Crying and Execrable Sinne of Wilfull and Premeditated Murther* (1621)—a collection of stories about adultery and murder. A secondary source has been identified as *Gerardo, the Unfortunate Spaniard*, a translation in 1622 by Leonard Digges of a Spanish tale.

While Reynolds' tale has all the main characters and is similar in broad outline, it lacks not only the motivation but the psychological complexity of the play. Most important, De Flores, a gallant young gentleman, is neither ugly nor repulsive to Beatrice nor does he blackmail her; their liaison is the result of a sudden and totally unreasonable attack of jealousy on Alsemero's part, three months after marriage. The idea of De Flores' blackmail and the need for a wedding-night substitution may well have been taken, as B. Lloyd argues,[1] from Digges' tale where the villain is a love-crazed Biscayner. The real difference between the play and its sources lies in the way in which the dramatists bring out, through the characters themselves, the inevitability of their actions, and thus transform an ill-motivated story of lust, murder, and revenge into one of the finest tragedies of the era.

[1] 'A Minor Source of *The Changeling*', M.L.R., XIX, 1924, 101–2.

THE PLAY

The theme of *The Changeling* is not unlike that of *The White Devil*. Like Vittoria, Beatrice-Joanna initiates the murder of those who stand in the way of her desires. Vittoria's words, as she was dying, might well have been Beatrice's:

> 'O my greatest sin lay in my blood.
> Now my blood pays for't.'

'Blood' or sensual desire, self-will and complete imperviousness to the rights of others—those are the qualities which bring about Beatrice's tragedy. But, unlike Webster, Middleton treats his heroine with a disenchanted realism which has no counterpart in the dazzled disapproval of the earlier playwright. Even as Webster condemns Vittoria he admires her; Middleton knows his heroine for what she is; he is, in Eliot's phrase, 'without fear, without sentiment, without prejudice'.

What should not, I think, be forgotten in criticizing *The Changeling* is that the responsibility for the murder of Piracquo and for the ensuing tragedy is Beatrice's. With the exception of Dr. N. W. Bawcutt, most modern critics have tended to stress the innocence of Beatrice as opposed to the callous wickedness of De Flores, the tool-villain who refuses to remain a tool in her hands. Professor Empson, for instance, describes Beatrice as 'morally a child such as the fairies can steal and fearing De Flores as a goblin';[1] Miss Gardner talks of 'the absolute contrast at the beginning and the identity at

---

[1] William Empson, *Some Versions of Pastoral* (1935), p. 52.

the close of Beatrice-Joanna and De Flores';[2] Professor
Ellis-Fermor refers to the 'essential innocence' of
Beatrice-Joanna and says that Middleton has 'grasped
the principle . . . that the more generously a nature is
endowed, especially perhaps a woman's, the more bitter
is its corruption if it is thwarted or maimed in the full
course of its development'.[3]

This seems to romanticize Middleton's heroine in a
way that he certainly did not, and to take away much
of the significance of the relationship between her and
De Flores. Beatrice is a beautiful and passionate young
woman but there is no indication that her nature is
unusually generously endowed and her 'innocence' is
rather ignorance of and disinterest in the motives and
feelings of others than a positive virtue. In Act I
Rowley is at pains to stress the driving-force, not only
of De Flores, but of Beatrice. Professor Ellis-Fermor
uses the phrase, 'a spoilt child', of Beatrice and it sums
up well the single-track quality of her mind. She is, in
fact, the wilful child of an imperious father. Vermandero
is set upon her match with Piracquo . . .

> 'I'll want
> My will else.'
>   (I, i, 219-20)

to which Beatrice murmurs, 'I shall want mine if you
do it.' De Flores is aware of the clash between his will
and hers. He describes her antipathy to him as causeless,
except for her 'peevish will' and the scene ends, with
the ominous threat from De Flores, 'I'll have my will.'
(I, i, 237.) This reiteration, in the opening scene, of the
word 'will' with its sexual overtones is, as Miss Bradbrook points out in *Themes and Conventions of Elizabe-*

---

[2] Helen Gardner, 'The Tragedy of Damnation', *Elizabethan Drama*
(ed. R. Kaufmann), 1961, p. 329. (Reprint of 1948 essay in *English
Studies.*)
[3] Una Ellis-Fermor, *The Jacobean Drama* (1936), p. 142.

than Tragedy, purposeful and is designed to bring out, not the contrast between the main characters, but their affinity.

This link between Beatrice and De Flores which is openly acknowledged by the end of the play is, though submerged at the beginning, none the less real. The violence of Beatrice's allergy to De Flores is, by its very nature, akin to passion. It is confessedly irrational. Alsemero speaks of loving and loathing in the same breath (I, i, 125) just as Shylock had—

> ... affection,
> Master of passion, sways it to the mood
> Of what it likes or loathes.
> 　　　*(Merchant of Venice* IV, i, 150–3)

and De Flores' defence of his obstinate wooing is based upon his belief that hatred and love are akin, that—

> 'Women have chid themselves abed to men.'
> 　　　　　　　　　　　　　(II, i, 88)

Beatrice's hatred of De Flores is more than simply the aversion of beauty from ugliness. For everyone else De Flores, like Iago, is 'honest'. It is not until Act V when Tomazo senses, instinctively, the guilt of his brother's murder upon De Flores, that he reacts violently against him and describes him as 'poison'. Before then, there are many approving references by other characters to him: 'kind De Flores'; 'kind and true'; 'honest'; 'wondrous honest'; 'good on all occasions'; 'worth 'em all'. It is not true, as Miss Bradbrook suggests, that the good people in the play have a natural antipathy to him. Beatrice is aware that she cannot substantiate her instinctive fear and dislike of him. She is as obsessed by her loathing of him as he is by his infatuation for her. Each is equally willing to inflict pain on the other. De Flores, fully aware of her feelings about him, persecutes her by making excuses to see her 'more than twenty times a day' and leaves her trembling with an emotion which she finds more disturbing than all her other passions. Beatrice, knowing that her father respects De Flores as a good servant, nevertheless ruthlessly determines to have him dismissed:

> 'The next good mood I find my father in,
> I'll get him quite discarded.'
>
>   (II, i, 92–3)

Beatrice's basic sin is her assumption that it is her privilege to manipulate others like puppets. It is the pitfall of the indulged only child. Such an assumption has tragic possibilities—even in comedy and even when the heroine acts out of the best of intentions, as in the case of Jane Austen's Emma, another indulged only daughter who, 'with unpardonable arrogance proposed to arrange everyone's destiny'. When the character is, like Beatrice, prompted wholly by selfish passion and prepared to make everyone 'low footsteps' to her marriage, it is almost inevitable that tragedy will follow —even without the complication of a De Flores. In an earlier play, *The Mayor of Queenborough*, Middleton wrote:

> ' 'tis her cunning
> The love of her own lust, which makes a woman
> Gallop down-hill as fearless as a drunkard.'
>
>   (II, iii, 167–9)

And there is the quality of the 'fearless drunkard' about Beatrice when in Act II she broaches the subject of Piracquo's murder to De Flores and starts the long down-hill gallop to their eventual damnation.

Once it is fully recognized that Beatrice is not merely the victim of De Flores' machinations, that, from the start, her a-morality matches his immorality, the growth of their relationship is seen to be far more complex and fascinating than if, in fact, he were 'the goblin' and she the 'child such as the fairies can steal'. Each is equally in the grip of passion; he, for Beatrice; she, for Alsemero. The reactions of Beatrice and Alsemero, on the other hand, to their violent infatuation for each other, point the contrast between them; Alsemero is completely (and traditionally) transformed by his sudden love—changed from a stoic and sceptic, a soldier always on the move into a love-sick wooer. But when he is sure that Beatrice returns his love his response is open and honourable; he is prepared to hazard his life for her, by a duel with Piracquo. Beatrice's horror at the risk to her lover is natural; what is unnatural in her is the swift sequence of thoughts which follow and culminate in her decision to have Piracquo eliminated:

> 'Blood-guiltiness becomes a fouler visage,
> [*aside*].—And now I think on one. I was to blame,
>   I ha' marr'd so good a market with my scorn;
>   'T had been done questionless; the ugliest creature
>   Creation fram'd for some use, yet to see
>   I could not mark so much where it should be!'
> *Alsemero*. Lady,—
> *Beatrice* [*aside*]. Why, men of art make much of poison,
>   Keep one to expel another; where was my
>   art?
> *Alsemero*. Lady, you hear not me.
> *Beatrice*.   I do especially, sir;
>   (II, ii, 40–8)

The down-hill gallop has started for Beatrice. She is in love not only with her own lust but with the economical ingenuity of her idea of using the poison of De Flores to expel the poison of Piracquo from her blood. In those few, frightening lines Beatrice is shown to be

impervious to the human rights, not only of Piracquo
and De Flores, but also, in her refusal to share her
thoughts with him, of Alsemero. It is ironical that
Beatrice still believes in the perfection of her relationship with Alsemero at the very moment of deceiving
him and treating him, too, like a counter. Beatrice has
been at pains to stress how different her love for
Alsemero is from her former love for Piracquo.

> 'Methinks I love now with the eyes of judgment,
> And see the way to merit, clearly see it.'
>
> (II, i, 13–14)

—but judgment of herself or others is a quality Beatrice
totally lacks. Even as she dismisses Alsemero, has him
hurried away by Diaphanta to leave the coast clear
for her interview with De Flores, the sham nature of
their relationship, their complete lack of knowledge of
each other, is suddenly and startlingly revealed to us.

This egotistical insulation of Beatrice is shown even
more clearly in her conversation with De Flores when
it is balanced by an equal egotism on his part. This
masterly scene (II, ii, 57 ff.) is one of the deepest
irony, as both pursue their own ends without reference
to the likelihood of the other's acquiescence. De Flores
is prepared to believe in Beatrice's barefaced flattery,
in her *volte-face* from 'thou standing toad-pool' to 'Oh
my De Flores' because it is bliss for him to believe in it.
'I'm up to the chin in heaven.' He does at least attempt
to appease his reason for her change of attitude by the
shrugged 'Some women are odd feeders', which is
consistent with his earlier defence of his persistence in
dogging her footsteps.

> 'I'll despair the less,
> Because there's daily precedents of bad faces
> Belov'd beyond all reason;'
>
> (II, i, 82–4)

Beatrice makes no similar attempt to gauge De Flores'
reasons for agreeing to her scheme. She has decided
his future actions for him:

> 'When the deed's done,
> I'll furnish thee with all things for thy flight;
> Thou may'st live bravely in another country.'
>
> (II, ii, 141–3)

and is unaware of De Flores' brushing this neat plan
aside:

> 'Ay, ay, we'll talk of that hereafter.'
>
> (II, ii, 144)

Beatrice leaves, still convinced of her ascendancy, but
it is De Flores who now holds the stage and who moves
into the central position with his ominous, exultant
soliloquy:

> 'O my blood!
> Methinks I feel her in my arms already' . . .
>
> (II, ii, 146–7)

Their mutual misunderstanding, unlike all the other
deceptions in the play, is short-lived. The great Act III,
scene iv, that magnificent éclaircissement on which
critics have spent so much praise, opens with Beatrice
congratulating herself on her most recent manipu-
lations, this time of her father and Alsemero (10–17),
and awaiting the report of De Flores. As in the earlier
interview the scene is close-packed with misconcep-
tions, contrasts and the most ruthless irony. Beatrice
sheds tears at the news of the death of her betrothed
but they are tears of joy. The 'tidings of the death of the
whole man' affect her less than the bloody actuality of
the severed finger with its token ring. De Flores, the
murderer, shocked and disillusioned by the offer of a
reward of gold, takes up the moral tone of injured
virtue:

' 'Twill hardly buy a capcase for one's conscience, though ...'

(III, iv, 44)

His gibes grow more bitter as Beatrice remains stubbornly uncomprehending of what has offended him and she steps up her offer of money:

> 'I'm in a labyrinth;
> What will content him?'

(III, iv, 71–2)

The cruellest blow for De Flores, after his recent hopes, is that Beatrice is patently incapable of imagining any relationship between them other than servant and mistress: for her he is an ugly monster fit for ugly deeds. Like a novice at chess she has worked out her moves without any reference to the manoeuvrability of her opponent and her reaction is one of appalled disbelief, when at last the checkmate comes and she realizes what he is demanding of her.

'Why, 'tis impossible thou canst be so wicked,'

(III, iv, 120)

—an extraordinarily revealing cry of pathos and horror, but one also of outraged chastity and self-righteousness, which stresses the gulf between them both in responsibility for the crime and in rank.

One of the most satisfying features, in fact, of the scene is its symbolic movement. It opens with Beatrice greeting De Flores as a princess her subject, and for the first hundred lines or so the difference in rank between them is assumed by Beatrice and ironically stressed by De Flores in his reiteration of 'lady', 'service', 'wages'. Then, in a flash, with De Flores' scornful reply to Beatrice's fine lady talk of 'modesty', the levelling process has begun.

'A woman dipp'd in blood, and talk of modesty!'

(III, iv, 126)

It is vain for Beatrice to remind him of the distance between them—

> 'You must forget your parentage to me:
> Y'are the deed's creature;'
>
> (III, iv, 136–7)

and De Flores and Beatrice now slang each other on equal terms:

> *Beatrice.*   With thee, foul villain?
> *De Flores.* Yes, my fair murd'ress;
>
> (III, iv, 140–1)

When, with a sudden capitulation to his power, Beatrice kneels with a pathetic plea for mercy, their rôles are completely reversed.

> 'Let me go poor unto my bed with honour,
> And I am rich in all things.'
>
> (III, iv, 158–9)

The note of wealth, which has echoed through all the scene is struck, in vain, for the last time. De Flores is magnificently adamant—

> 'Can you weep Fate from its determin'd purpose?
> So soon may you weep me.'
>
> (III, iv, 162–3)

And when, as her conqueror, he stoops to raise her to stand enclosed in his triumphant embrace, the movement is complete. 'My partner she shall be.' It is on a final masterly touch of condescending tenderness that Middleton ends the scene.

> 'Las, how the turtle pants! Thou'lt love anon
> What thou so fear'st and faint'st to venture on.'
>
> (III, iv, 170–1)

Act IV begins with a sardonic contrast between the appearance of happy bustle in the wedding procession, with Beatrice in the full panoply of virgin bride, and the reality of the solitary soliloquy which follows it. De

Flores has been true to his name; Beatrice is now de-flowered. Her first line, 'This fellow has undone me endlessly' has a blunt, coarsened quality about it. No longer is Beatrice remote from the consequences of her sin and she can think of nothing but preserving from discovery the loss of her chastity. Irrevocably one action dictates the next. With ingenuity and cunning, inde-pendent of any assistance from De Flores, she sets about outwitting her new husband, counterfeiting virginity to delude 'a cunning gamester', as she now describes him, arranging for the substitution of her maid in her bridal bed. The humiliation of Beatrice as she waits and listens in the darkness, outside her own bedroom door, while Diaphanta lies in Alsemero's arms; her desperation as the hours tick past and dis-covery seems inevitable; the pathetic loneliness of her reply to De Flores' impatient question:

> ... who'd trust
>
> A waiting-woman?
>
> **Beatrice.**   I must trust somebody.
>
> (V, i, 14–15)

all these would move more pity if it were not clear that the 'spiritual degradation' of Beatrice is only partly a result of her liaison with De Flores. Beatrice's decision to have Diaphanta killed is no more—and no less—callous and cold-blooded than her earlier resolve to have Piracquo eliminated. In a few words she dismisses Diaphanta from life—'she pays dearly for't'—a pawn no longer to be allowed to threaten the queen. Ruth-lessness, egotism, selfishness—these qualities are not new in Beatrice. What is new is her cynicism, her hardened recklessness and her growing attachment to De Flores.

They are now partners in every sense. De Flores needs no telling to kill Diaphanta. Their instincts and impulses run in the same current. They speak the same language:

> De Flores. . . . I could have help'd you to an apothecary's
> daughter,
>   Would have fall'n off before eleven, and thank'd
>   you too.
> Beatrice. Oh me, not yet? This whore forgets herself.
>
>   (V, i, 21–3)

When Beatrice praises his murder-plan in terms which hint once again at the condescending servant-mistress relationship, De Flores is brutally quick to stress their new sexual alliance.

> Beatrice.   I'm forc'd to love thee now,
>   'Cause thou provid'st so carefully for my honour.
> De Flores. 'Slid, it concerns the safety of us both,
>   Our pleasure and continuance.
>
>   (V, i, 47–50)

Beatrice has come a long way from the young girl who spoke of Alsemero as 'a true deserver', because of his idealistic allegiance to her. It is the practical quality in De Flores, as he sets about saving the situation—a scene not without a certain grim humour—which arouses her admiration. As she watches him ringing the fire bell, organizing the servants with their hooks, buckets and ladders, loading his fire-arm to despatch Diaphanta, she thrills to his efficiency and even as Diaphanta substitutes for her in her bed, she replaces Alsemero by De Flores in her heart:

> Beatrice. Already! How rare is that man's speed!
>   How heartily he serves me! His face loathes one,
>   But look upon his care, who would not love him?
>   The east is not more beauteous than his service.
>
>   (V, i, 69–72)

'Service' implies not only serving-man but lover, and it is with a cynical boldness which takes even De Flores

aback that she claims from her father a reward for the
services of this 'wondrous necessary man'. So that the
reward of gold which De Flores had refused from
Beatrice for the first murder comes his way, by proxy,
for the second.

By the end of Act IV, then, Beatrice and De Flores
are indeed 'twins of mischief' and in Act V Rowley
handles with a fine gravity the death-scene of two
damned souls. There is no blurring of moral issues in
this last scene. De Flores and Beatrice-Joanna have for
some time been carrying their guilt around with them
like a tangible presence—as De Flores realizes when
Tomazo senses the evil in him.

> 'Guilt must not walk so near his lodge again;
> He came near me now.'
>
> (V, ii, 41-2)

Alsemero, too, has found that De Flores' 'black mask'
matches the 'cunning face', the reality underlying
Beatrice's visor—although to the end Beatrice continues
to dissemble, admitting only to murder and not to what
she thinks, in Schoenbaum's phrase, the more 'socially
unacceptable' sin of adultery. Her values are still ego-
centric; she is still more concerned with concealing
the violation of her own body than the destruction of
another's;

> 'Remember I am true unto your bed.'
>
> (V, iii, 82)

And even although Alsemero shames her by his reply:

> 'The bed itself's a charnel, the sheets shrouds
> For murder'd carcasses.'
>
> (V, iii, 83-4)

she still has the tenacity to shriek her denial from the
closet, when she overhears De Flores call her a whore:

> 'He lies, the villain does bely me!'
>
> (V, iii, 110)

Many of the familiar features of revenge tragedy are present in the final scene of *The Changeling*, many echoes of Webster in particular: the violent deaths, the tool-villain's delight in a task well accomplished, 'her honour's prize was my reward', the evil-doer's desire to be 'laid by and never thought of'—the prevailing atmosphere of fatality:

> 'Beneath the stars, upon yon meteor
> Ever hung my fate,'
>
> (V, iii, 154–5)

But although here, as elsewhere in the play, we are often reminded of Webster the final impression of the dénouement is very different. There is no admiration for the way in which the sinners face death, no feeling of doubt as to the moral strength of those who survive them. Rowley is at pains to recall the sacrilege of the temple-wooing, and drives home the point in one religious image after another—'lips', 'saint', 'devils', 'broken rib', 'serpent'. Miss Bradbrook has pointed out the persistence of poison imagery throughout the play and in Beatrice's last speech there is a cleansing quality of truth and self-knowledge at last. De Flores has been the poison in her blood as she, in her own way, has been his—'I lov'd this woman in spite of her heart'—and for two such hopelessly infected people, oblivion and loss of identity can be the only answer. There is a strange relief in the starkness of Beatrice's assessment of the situation: the masks and visors are finally down:

> 'Oh, come not near me, sir, I shall defile you;
> I am that of your blood was taken from you
> For your better health; look no more upon't,
> But cast it to the ground regardlessly,
> Let the common sewer take it from distinction.'
>
> (V, iii, 149–53)

There is no doubt that the bare style of the poetry, what Professor Ellis-Fermor describes as 'the pitiless abstemiousness' of Middleton's verse, contributes greatly to the total effect of the play. There is very little use of imagery, no dazzling poetic flashes of illumination as in Webster, whose lines, detached from their context, can have an autonomous splendour:

> What would it pleasure me to have my throat cut
> With diamonds? or to be smothered
> With cassia? or to be shot to death with pearls?
>
> *The Duchess of Malfi* (IV, ii, 219–21)

There is little like this in Middleton. Very occasionally the lines can stand alone—as in the impressive and irrevocable beat of

> 'Can you weep Fate from its determin'd purpose?
> So soon may you weep me.'
>
> (III, iv, 162–3)

of Beatrice's dying speech. But most of the unforgettable phrases gain their strength and significance from their inevitability in their context—'Y'are the deeds creature'; 'A wondrous necessary man'; 'Blood guiltiness becomes a fouler visage'; 'A woman dipp'd in blood, and talk of modesty'; 'Here comes the man goes supperless to bed.' In their setting, these spare direct statements have a compelling force, complicated often by deeply emotional or ironic undertones. Words are not used by Middleton for the embellishment of an idea; they are the idea. When he is writing at his best, form is completely instinct with matter.

It is not surprising that most of the criticism of *The Changeling* should have centred upon the psychological complexity of the relationship between Beatrice-Joanna and De Flores. Compared with the two sinners, the remaining characters in the play are conventional figures. Professor Schoenbaum has described the play as 'a flawed masterpiece' and cites two flaws, in particular, the virginity tests and the sub-plot.

The first, Alsemero's virginity tests, which take up a large part of Act IV, many critics have found to be distasteful or fantastic. They can probably best be tolerated by considering them, as Dr. Bawcutt suggests, as 'symbolic of the kind of problem Beatrice has constantly to face now that she has committed herself to evil'.[4] Just as Volpone's bastard family 'make visible his inner defects' (J. J. Enck), so the mumbo-jumbo with the test-tubes and vials brings home to the audience the actual fact of Beatrice's loss of virginity—and to Beatrice herself the immediate physical consequences of her initial sin. It seems, too, to emphasize the inadequacy of the relationship for which so much has been hazarded, the complete lack of trust between Alsemero and Beatrice—so that the former requires test-tube proof of his wife's purity, the latter triumphs in deceiving him.

Until lately the sub-plot received short shrift from commentators. Swinburne condemned it as 'very stupid, rather coarse and almost vulgar':[5] Oliphant observed: 'It is a pity that the silly underplot should have given its name to a tragedy that ranks among the very finest in the language';[6] T. S. Eliot talked of its 'nauseousness'[7] and Professor Ellis-Fermor suggested that it could be omitted without violence to the rest. But the relevance of the sub-plot to the main theme has been fully

---

[4] N. W. Bawcutt, *The Changeling* (The Revels Plays) (1958), p. lvii.

[5] A. Swinburne, *Thomas Middleton* (The Mermaid Series) (1887). Introduction, p. xxxiii.

[6] E. H. C. Oliphant, *Shakespeare and his Fellow Dramatists* (1929), II, 901.

[7] T. S. Eliot, *The Use of Poetry and The Use of Criticism* (1933), p. 41.

demonstrated in more recent analyses by Professor
Empson, Miss Bradbrook and Dr. Bawcutt. The situation of Isabella, the wife of the asylum keeper Alibius,
parallels in some respects that of Beatrice-Joanna. She
is tempted to be untrue to her husband by the two
disguised lovers Antonio and Franciscus, and, like De
Flores, Lollio tries to blackmail her to cut himself in on
the bargain. The lovers, in their note of madness,
bring out the unreasoning quality of love—'This is
love's tame madness'—and the two plots are deliber-
ately linked by the fact that Antonio and Franciscus are
suspected of the murder of Piracquo. There are many
verbal echoes (e.g. the barley-brake reference by De
Flores which reminds us of the madmen's game) and
there is the final, shared imagery of change and transformation (V, iii, 196 *seq.*). Unlike Beatrice, Isabella
is impervious to temptation and Alibius escapes
cuckoldry so that the sub-plot provides a through-
the-looking-glass, madhouse reflection of the main
theme.

For most readers, however, the serious charge
against the sub-plot is not irrelevance so much as lack
of interest. Quite clearly Rowley, with his partiality for
clowns, wrote the changeling's part so that the actor
who played it had considerable scope for horse-play and
stage-business. The title-part of Antonio, the fool
among the madmen, twirling his bauble, mouthing out
his *double-entendres*, took the fancy of contemporary
audiences and ensured the success of the play. The
sub-plot gives the impression, in fact, of being pri-
marily a vehicle for clowning and will not stand up to
too serious examination as a counterpart of the main
plot, although it does provide a grotesque commentary
upon certain of its features. Isabella remains true to
her marriage vows but Alibius is an unattractive charac-

ter, battening off his charges, as his wife contemptuously points out:

> 'Y'have a fine trade on't,
> Madmen and fools are a staple commodity.'
>
> (III, iii, 284-5)

She is aware that he is a 'jealous coxcomb' who keeps her prisoner, 'a bounden servant', for fear of being cuckolded—a fate he would certainly not have avoided in a Middleton comedy. So that while it is true that her astringent comments serve to bring out the close alliance of love and madness in both plots, her own loveless marriage is as mad in its own way. She shows good sense and a level head in rebuffing the attempts on her virtue of her 'lunatic lovers', but she is clearly so little involved with either suitors or husband that the comparison with Beatrice is only a superficial one of situation. In fact, while the anti-masque quality of the sub-plot is undeniable, it is difficult to make out a case for it as either coherent or appealing.

FURTHER READING

R. H. Barker — *Thomas Middleton* (New York, 1958)

M. C. Bradbrook — *Themes and Conventions of Elizabethan Tragedy* (Cambridge, 1935)

Fredson Bowers — *Elizabethan Revenge Tragedy* (Princeton, 1940)

T. S. Eliot — 'Thomas Middleton', *Selected Essays* (London, 1932)

Una Ellis-Fermor — *The Jacobean Drama* (London, 1936)

William Empson — *Some Versions of Pastoral* (London, 1935)

Helen Gardner — 'The Tragedy of Damnation', *Elizabethan Drama* (ed. R. Kaufmann) New York (1961)

David Holmes — *The Art of Thomas Middleton* (Oxford, 1970)

Christopher Ricks — '*The Moral and Poetical Structure of The Changeling*', *Essays in Criticism* X (July 1960)

Samuel Schoenbaum — *Middleton's Tragedies* (New York, 1955)

THE

CHANGELING:

As it was Acted (with great Applause)
at the Privat house in DRURY-LANE,
and *Salisbury Court.*

Written by {*THOMAS MIDLETON,*
           and
           WILLIAM ROWLEY.} Gent.

Never Printed before.

LONDON,

Printed for HUMPHREY MOSELEY, and are to
be sold at his shop at the sign of the *Princes-Arms*
in St. *Pauls* Church-yard, 1653.

DRAMATIS PERSONAE

Vermandero. Father to Beatrice.
Tomazo de Piracquo. A noble lord.
Alonzo de Piracquo. His brother, suitor to Beatrice.
Alsemero. A nobleman, afterwards married to Beatrice.
Jasperino. His friend.
Alibius. A jealous doctor.
Lollio. His man.
Pedro. Friend to Antonio.
Antonio. The changeling.
Franciscus. The counterfeit madman.
De Flores. Servant to Vermandero.
Madmen.
Servants.

Beatrice. Daughter to Vermandero.
Diaphanta. Her waiting-woman.
Isabella. Wife to Alibius.

The Scene: Alicant.

3

An asterisk denotes that a fuller annotation will be found in the **Critical Notes** on pages 94–100.

THE CHANGELING

Act I, Scene i

Enter ALSEMERO.

Alsemero. 'Twas in the temple where I first beheld
    her,   *
And now again the same; what omen yet
Follows of that? None but imaginary.
Why should my hopes or fate be timorous?
The place is holy, so is my intent;   5
I love her beauties to the holy purpose,
And that, methinks, admits comparison
With man's first creation, the place blest,
And is his right home back, if he achieve it.
The church hath first begun our interview,   10
And that's the place must join us into one,
So there's beginning and perfection too.

Enter JASPERINO.

Jasperino. Oh, sir, are you here? Come, the wind's fair
    with you,
Y'are like to have a swift and pleasant passage.
Alsemero. Sure, y'are deceived, friend, 'tis contrary   15
In my best judgment.
Jasperino.   What, for Malta?
If you could buy a gale amongst the witches,
They could not serve you such a lucky pennyworth
As comes a' God's name.
Alsemero.   Even now I observ'd

The Scene. A street in Alicant, a seaport in Valencia.
6 *holy purpose* marriage   8 *place blest* Eden
17 *gale . . . witches* popular belief cf. Macbeth I, iii
19 *a' God's name* without payment

20   The temple's vane to turn full in my face,
      I know 'tis against me.
          Jasperino.   Against you?
      Then you know not where you are.
          Alsemero.   Not well, indeed.
          Jasperino. Are you not well, sir?
          Alsemero.   Yes, Jasperino;
      Unless there be some hidden malady
      Within me, that I understand not.
25   *Jasperino.*   And that
      I begin to doubt, sir. I never knew
      Your inclination to travels at a pause
      With any cause to hinder it, till now.
      Ashore you were wont to call your servants up,
30   And help to trap your horses for the speed;
      At sea I have seen you weigh the anchor with 'em,
      Hoist sails for fear to lose the foremost breath,
      Be in continual prayers for fair winds,
      And have you chang'd your orisons?
          Alsemero.   No, friend,
35   I keep the same church, same devotion.
          Jasperino. Lover I'm sure y'are none, the stoic was
      Found in you long ago. Your mother nor
      Best friends, who have set snares of beauty—ay,
      And choice ones too—could never trap you that way.
      What might be the cause?
40   *Alsemero.*   Lord, how violent
      Thou art! I was but meditating of
      Somewhat I heard within the temple.
          Jasperino. Is this violence? 'Tis but idleness
      Compar'd with your haste yesterday.
45   *Alsemero.* I'm all this while a-going, man.

                    Enter Servants.

27 *inclination* ed. (inclinations *Q*)
30 *trap . . . speed* hasten departure by harnessing horses

Jasperino. Backwards, I think, sir. Look, your ser-
    vants.

  1 Servant. The seamen call; shall we board your
    trunks?

Alsemero. No, not today.

Jasperino. 'Tis the critical day, it seems, and the sign
    in Aquarius.   50

  2 Servant [*aside*]. We must not to sea today; this
    smoke will bring forth fire!

Alsemero. Keep all on shore; I do not know the end,
(Which needs I must do) of an affair in hand
Ere I can go to sea.

  1 Servant.   Well, your pleasure.   55

  2 Servant [*aside*]. Let him e'en take his leisure too,
    we are safer on land.   *Exeunt* SERVANTS.

Enter BEATRICE, DIAPHANTA, *and* SERVANTS. [ALSEMERO
greets BEATRICE *and kisses her.*]

Jasperino [*aside*]. How now! The laws of the Medes
are changed sure! Salute a woman? He kisses too;
wonderful! Where learnt he this? And does it perfectly
too; in my conscience he ne'er rehearsed it before. Nay,   60
go on, this will be stranger and better news at Valencia
than if he had ransomed half Greece from the Turk.

Beatrice. You are a scholar, sir?

Alsemero.   A weak one, lady.

Beatrice. Which of the sciences is this love you speak
    of?   65

Alsemero. From your tongue, I take it to be music.

Beatrice. You are skilful in't, can sing at first sight.

Alsemero. And I have show'd you all my skill at once.
I want more words to express me further,
And must be forc'd to repetition: 70
I love you dearly.

50 *Aquarius* propitious for sea-travel

Beatrice.   Be better advis'd sir;
Our eyes are sentinels unto our judgments,
And should give certain judgment what they see;
But they are rash sometimes and tell us wonders

75 Of common things, which, when our judgments find,
They then can check the eyes and call them blind.

Alsemero. But I am further, lady; yesterday
Was mine eyes' employment, and hither now
They brought my judgment, where are both agreed.

80 Both houses then consenting, 'tis agreed;
Only there wants the confirmation
By the hand royal—that's your part, lady.

Beatrice. Oh, there's one above me, sir. [*aside.*] For
          five days past
To be recall'd! Sure, mine eyes were mistaken,

85 This was the man was meant me—That he should come
So near his time, and miss it!

Jasperino [*aside*]. We might have come by the carriers
from Valencia, I see, and saved all our sea provision;
we are at farthest sure. Methinks I should do something

90 too; I meant to be a venturer in this voyage. Yonder's
* another vessel, I'll board her; if she be lawful prize,
down goes her top sail!   [*Approaches* DIAPHANTA.]

Enter DE FLORES.

De Flores. Lady, your father—
Beatrice.   Is in health, I hope.
De Flores. Your eye shall instantly instruct you, lady.
He's coming hitherward.

95 *Beatrice.*   What needed then
Your duteous preface? I had rather
He had come unexpected; you must stall
A good presence with unnecessary blabbing;
And how welcome for your part you are,

80 *Both houses* Lords and Commons   97 *stall* forestall

I'm sure you know.

  De Flores [*aside*]. Will't never mend, this scorn,   100
One side nor other? Must I be enjoin'd
To follow still whilst she flies from me? Well,
Fates do your worst, I'll please myself with sight
Of her, at all opportunities,
If but to spite her anger; I know she had   105
Rather see me dead than living, and yet
She knows no cause for't but a peevish will.

  Alsemero. You seem'd displeased, lady, on the sudden.

  Beatrice. Your pardon, sir, 'tis my infirmity;
Nor can I other reason render you   110
Than his or hers, of some particular thing
They must abandon as a deadly poison,
Which to a thousand other tastes were wholesome;
Such to mine eyes is that same fellow there,
The same that report speaks of the basilisk.   115

  Alsemero. This is a frequent frailty in our nature;
There's scarce a man amongst a thousand sound,   *
But hath his imperfection: one distastes
The scent of roses, which to infinites
Most pleasing is, and odoriferous;   120
One oil, the enemy of poison,
Another wine, the cheerer of the heart,
And lively refresher of the countenance.
Indeed, this fault, if so it be, is general;
There's scarce a thing but is both lov'd and loath'd;   125
Myself, I must confess, have the same frailty.

  Beatrice. And what may be your poison, sir? I am
  bold with you.

  Alsemero. What might be your desire, perhaps; a
  cherry.   *

111 *his or hers* **this** or **that**
115 *basilisk* reputed to have a killing glance
119 *infinites* many people
128 *What* ed. (And what *Q*)

Beatrice. I am no enemy to any creature
130 My memory has, but yon gentleman.
    Alsemero. He does ill to tempt your sight, if he knew
      it.
    Beatrice. He cannot be ignorant of that, sir,
I have not spar'd to tell him so; and I want
To help myself, since he's a gentleman
135 In good respect with my father, and follows him.
    Alsemero. He's out of his place then now.

                      [They talk apart.]

    Jasperino. I am a mad wag, wench.
    Diaphanta. So methinks; but for your comfort I can
tell you, we have a doctor in the city that undertakes
140 the cure of such.
    Jasperino. Tush, I know what physic is best for the
state of mine own body.
    Diaphanta. 'Tis scarce a well governed state, I believe.
    Jasperino. I could show thee such a thing with an
145 ingredient that we two would compound together, and
if it did not tame the maddest blood i' th' town for two
hours after, I'll ne'er profess physic again.
    Diaphanta. A little poppy, sir, were good to cause you
      sleep.
    Jasperino. Poppy? I'll give thee a pop i' th' lips for
150 that first, and begin there; poppy is one simple indeed,
* and cuckoo (what you call't) another. I'll discover no
more now, another time I'll show thee all.
    Beatrice. My father, sir.

        Enter VERMANDERO *and* SERVANTS.

    Vermandero.   Oh, Joanna, I came to meet thee;
Your devotion's ended?
    Beatrice.   For this time, sir.—

133 *want* am unable   139 *doctor* Alibius
150 *simple* remedy from plant or herb
151 *cuckoo (what you call't)* cuckoo pintle-root

[*aside*]. I shall change my saint, I fear me; I find   155
A giddy turning in me.—Sir, this while
I am beholding to this gentleman,
Who left his own way to keep me company,
And in discourse I find him much desirous
To see your castle; he hath deserv'd it, sir,   160
If ye please to grant it.
   Vermandero.   With all my heart, sir.
Yet there's an article between, I must know
Your country; we use not to give survey
Of our chief strengths to strangers; our citadels
Are plac'd conspicuous to outward view,   165
On promonts' tops; but within are secrets.
   Alsemero. A Valencian, sir.
   Vermandero.   A Valencian?
That's native, sir; of what name, I beseech you?
   Alsemero. Alsemero, sir.
   Vermandero.   Alsemero; not the son
Of John de Alsemero?
   Alsemero.   The same, sir.   170
   Vermandero. My best love bids you welcome.
   Beatrice [*aside*].   He was wont
To call me so, and then he speaks a most
Unfeigned truth.
   Vermandero.   Oh, sir, I knew your father;
We two were in acquaintance long ago,
Before our chins were worth Iulan down,   * 175
And so continued till the stamp of time
Had coin'd us into silver. Well, he's gone;
A good soldier went with him.
   Alsemero. You went together in that, sir.
   Vermandero. No, by Saint Jaques, I came behind him   180
Yet I have done somewhat too; an unhappy day

162 *article* condition
172 *To call me so* Beatrice, his best love
175 *Iulan down* first growth of the beard

Swallowed him at last at Gibraltar
In fight with those rebellious Hollanders,
Was it not so?
    Alsemero.   Whose death I had reveng'd,
185 Or follow'd him in fate, had not the late league
Prevented me.
    Vermandero. Ay, ay, 'twas time to breathe.—
Oh, Joanna, I should ha' told thee news,
I saw Piracquo lately.
    Beatrice [aside].   That's ill news.
    Vermandero. He's hot preparing for this day of tri-
       umph:
Thou must be a bride within this sevennight.
190   *Alsemero [aside].*   Ha!
    Beatrice. Nay, good sir, be not so violent; with speed
I cannot render satisfaction
Unto the dear companion of my soul,
Virginity, whom I thus long have liv'd with,
195 And part with it so rude and suddenly;
Can such friends divide, never to meet again,
Without a solemn farewell?
    Vermandero.   Tush, tush! There's a toy.
    Alsemero [aside]. I must now part, and never meet
       again
With any joy on earth.—Sir, your pardon,
My affairs call on me.
200   *Vermandero.*   How, sir? By no means;
Not chang'd so soon, I hope. You must see my
    castle,
And her best entertainment ere we part;
I shall think myself unkindly used else.
Come, come, let's on; I had good hope your stay
205 Had been a while with us in Alicant;
I might have bid you to my daughter's wedding.

185 *late league* armistice 1609–21, **between Spain and Netherlands**

Alsemero [*aside*]. He means to feast me, and poisons
    me beforehand.—
I should be dearly glad to be there, sir,
Did my occasions suit as I could wish.

    Beatrice. I shall be sorry if you be not there   210
When it is done, sir;—but not so suddenly.

    Vermandero. I tell you, sir, the gentleman's complete,
A courtier and a gallant, enrich'd
With many fair and noble ornaments;
I would not change him for a son-in-law   215
For any he in Spain, the proudest he,
And we have great ones, that you know.

    Alsemero.   He's much
Bound to you, sir.

    Vermandero.   He shall be bound to me,
As fast as this tie can hold him; I'll want
My will else.

    Beatrice [*aside*]. I shall want mine if you do it.   220

    Vermandero. But come, by the way I'll tell you more
    of him.

    Alsemero [*aside*]. How shall I dare to venture in his
    castle,
When he discharges murderers at the gate?
But I must on, for back I cannot go.

    Beatrice [*aside*]. Not this serpent gone yet? [*Drops a*
glove.]

    Vermandero.   Look, girl, thy glove's fall'n.   225
Stay, stay; De Flores, help a little.

[*Exeunt* VERMANDERO, ALSEMERO, JASPERINO *and* SER-
VANTS.]

    De Flores.   Here, lady. [*Offers the glove.*]

    Beatrice. Mischief on your officious forwardness!
Who bade you stoop? They touch my hand no
    more.

223 *murderers* small cannon

There! For t'other's sake I part with this;
> [*Takes off the other glove and throws it down.*]

230 Take 'em and draw thine own skin off with 'em.
> *Exeunt* [BEATRICE *and* DIAPHANTA.]

> *De Flores.* Here's a favour come, with a mischief!
> Now I know

She had rather wear my pelt tann'd in a pair
Of dancing pumps than I should thrust my fingers
Into her sockets here; I know she hates me,

235 Yet cannot choose but love her;
No matter; if but to vex her, I'll haunt her still;
Though I get nothing else, I'll have my will.   *Exit.*

Act I, Scene ii

Enter ALIBIUS *and* LOLLIO.

Alibius. Lollio, I must trust thee with a secret,
But thou must keep it.

> *Lollio.* I was ever close to a secret, sir.

> *Alibius.* The diligence that I have found in thee,

5 The care and industry already past,
Assures me of thy good continuance.
Lollio, I have a wife.

> *Lollio.* Fie, sir, 'tis too late to keep her secret, she's
> known to be married all the town and country over.

> *Alibius.* Thou goest too fast, my Lollio; that know-

10 ledge
I allow no man can be barr'd it;
But there is a knowledge which is nearer,
Deeper, and sweeter, Lollio.

> *Lollio.* Well, sir, let us handle that between you and I.

15 *Alibius.* 'Tis that I go about, man. Lollio,
My wife is young.

> *Lollio.* So much the worse to be kept secret, sir.

Scene, as for all the sub-plot, in Alibius' mad-house.

Alibius. Why, now thou meet'st the substance of the
    point;
I am old, Lollio.

Lollio. No, sir, 'tis I am old Lollio.   20

Alibius. Yet why may not this concord and sympa-
    thize?
Old trees and young plants often grow together,
Well enough agreeing.

Lollio. Ay, sir, but the old trees raise themselves   ✱
higher and broader than the young plants.   25

Alibius. Shrewd application! There's the fear, man:
I would wear my ring on my own finger;
Whilst it is borrowed it is none of mine,
But his that useth it.

Lollio. You must keep it on still then; if it but lie by, 30
One or other will be thrusting into't.

Alibius. Thou conceiv'st me, Lollio; here thy watch-
    ful eye
Must have employment; I cannot always be
At home.

Lollio. I dare swear you cannot.   35

Alibius. I must look out.

Lollio. I know't; you must look out, 'tis every man's
    case.

Alibius. Here, I do say, must thy employment be:
To watch her treadings, and in my absence   40
Supply my place.

Lollio. I'll do my best, sir; yet surely I cannot see
who you should have cause to be jealous of.

Alibius. Thy reason for that, Lollio? 'Tis a comfort-
able question.

Lollio. We have but two sorts of people in the house,   45
and both under the whip, that's fools and madmen;
the one has not wit enough to be knaves, and the other
not knavery enough to be fools.

Alibius. Ay, those are all my patients, Lollio.

50 I do profess the cure of either sort;
My trade, my living 'tis, I thrive by it;
But here's the care that mixes with my thrift:
The daily visitants, that come to see
My brainsick patients, I would not have
55 To see my wife: gallants I do observe
Of quick enticing eyes, rich in habits,
Of stature and proportion very comely:
These are most shrewd temptations, Lollio.

Lollio. They may be easily answered, sir; if they come
60 to see the fools and madmen, you and I may serve the
turn, and let my mistress alone, she's of neither sort.

Alibius. 'Tis a good ward; indeed, come they to see
Our madmen or our fools, let 'em see no more
Than what they come for; by that consequent
65 They must not see her, I'm sure she's no fool.

Lollio. And I'm sure she's no madman.

Alibius. Hold that buckler fast, Lollio, my trust
Is on thee, and I account it firm and strong.
What hour is't, Lollio?

70 *Lollio.* Towards belly-hour, sir.

Alibius. Dinner time? Thou mean'st twelve o'clock?

Lollio. Yes, sir, for every part has his hour: we wake
at six and look about us, that's eye-hour; at seven we
should pray, that's knee-hour; at eight walk, that's leg-
75 hour; at nine gather flowers and pluck a rose, that's
nose-hour; at ten we drink, that's mouth-hour; at
eleven lay about us for victuals, that's hand-hour; at
twelve go to dinner, that's belly-hour.

Alibius. Profoundly, Lollio! It will be long
80 Ere all thy scholars learn this lesson, and
I did look to have a new one entered;—stay,

62 *ward* security
75 *pluck a rose* Elizabethan euphemism: pass water

I think my expectation is come home.

Enter PEDRO, *and* ANTONIO *like an idiot.*

Pedro. Save you, sir; my business speaks itself,
This sight takes off the labour of my tongue.
Alibius. Ay, ay, sir, 'tis plain enough; you mean him   85
for my patient.
Pedro. And if your pains prove but commodious, to
give but some little strength to his sick and weak part
of nature in him, these are but patterns [*gives him
money*] to show you of the whole pieces that will follow   90
to you, beside the charge of diet, washing and other
necessaries fully defrayed.
Alibius. Believe it, sir, there shall no care be wanting.
Lolliol. Sir, an officer in this place may deserve something; the trouble will pass through my hands.   95
Pedro. 'Tis fit something should come to your hands
then, sir.
[*Gives him money.*]
Lollio. Yes, sir, 'tis I must keep him sweet, and read
to him; what is his name?
Pedro. His name is Antonio; marry, we use but half   100
to him, only Tony.
Lollio. Tony, Tony; 'tis enough, and a very good
name for a fool; what's your name, Tony?
Antonio. He, he, he! well, I thank you, cousin; he,
he, he!   105
Lollio. Good boy! hold up your head. He can laugh;
I perceive by that he is no beast.
Pedro. Well, sir,
If you can raise him but to any height,
Any degree of wit, might he attain,   110
(As I might say) to creep but on all four

87 *commodious* useful   98 *sweet* clean
107 *no beast* classical belief that laughter distinguished man from
beasts

Towards the chair of wit, or walk on crutches,
'Twould add an honour to your worthy pains,
And a great family might pray for you,
115 To which he should be heir, had he discretion
To claim and guide his own; assure you, sir,
He is a gentleman.

Lollio. Nay, there's nobody doubted that; at first sight I knew him for a gentleman, he looks no other yet.

Pedro. Let him have good attendance and sweet
120   lodging.

Lollio. As good as my mistress lies in, sir; and as you allow us time and means, we can raise him to the higher degree of discretion.

Pedro. Nay, there shall no cost want, sir.

125 *Lollio.* He will hardly be stretched up to the wit of a magnifico.

Pedro. Oh no, that's not to be expected, far shorter will be enough.

Lollio. I'll warrant you I'll make him fit to bear
130 office in five weeks; I'll undertake to wind him up to the wit of constable.

Pedro. If it be lower than that it might serve turn.

Lollio. No, fie, to level him with a headborough, beadle, or watchman were but little better than he is;
135 constable I'll able him; if he do some to be a justice afterwards, let him thank the keeper. Or I'll go further with you; say I do bring him up to my own pitch, say I make him as wise as myself.

Pedro. Why, there I would have it.

140 *Lollio.* Well, go to; either I'll be as arrant a fool as he, or he shall be as wise as I, and then I think 'twill serve his turn.

Pedro. Nay, I do like thy wit passing well.

129 *you I'll* ed. (you *Q*)
131 *constable* proverbially stupid   135 *able* qualify, make fit

Lollio. Yes, you may; yet if I had not been a fool, I
had had more wit than I have too; remember what 145
state you find me in.

Pedro. I will, and so leave you; your best cares, I
    beseech you. [*Exit* PEDRO.]

Alibius. Take you none with you; leave 'em all with
    us.

Antonio. Oh, my cousin's gone, cousin, cousin, oh! 150

Lollio. Peace, peace, Tony; you must not cry, child,
you must be whipped if you do; your cousin is here
still; I am your cousin, Tony.

Antonio. He, he! then I'll not cry, if thou be'st my
    cousin; he, he, he! 155

Lollio. I were best try his wit a little, that I may know
    what form to place him in.

Alibius. Ay, do, Lollio, do.

Lollio. I must ask him easy questions at first; Tony,
how many true fingers has a tailor on his right hand? 160

Antonio. As many as on his left, cousin.

Lollio. Good; and how many on both?

Antonio. Two less than a deuce, cousin.

Lollio. Very well answered; I come to you again,
cousin Tony; how many fools goes to a wise man? 165

Antonio. Forty in a day sometimes, cousin.

Lollio. Forty in a day? How prove you that?

Antonio. All that fall out amongst themselves, and go
    to a lawyer to be made friends.

Lollio. A parlous fool! He must sit in the fourth form 170
at least, I perceive that; I come again, Tony; how many
knaves make an honest man?

Antonio. I know not that, cousin.

Lollio. No, the question is too hard for you: I'll tell
you, cousin, there's three knaves may make an honest 175
man, a sergeant, a jailer, and a beadle; the sergeant

160 *true* trustworthy   165 *goes to* (1) make. (2) visit

catches him, the jailer holds him and the beadle lashes
him; and if he be not honest then, the hangman must
cure him.

180   *Antonio.* Ha, ha, ha! That's fine sport, cousin.

    Alibius. This was too deep a question for the fool,
Lollio.

    Lollio. Yes, this might have served yourself, though I
say't; once more, and you shall go play, Tony.

185   *Antonio.* Ay, play at push-pin, cousin; ha, he!

    Lollio. So thou shalt; say how many fools are here—

    Antonio. Two, cousin, thou and I.

    Lollio. Nay, y'are too forward there, Tony; mark my
question: how many fools and knaves are here? A fool

190 before a knave, a fool behind a knave, between every
two fools a knave; how many fools, how many knaves?

    Antonio. I never learnt so far, cousin.

    Alibius. Thou putt'st too hard questions to him,
Lollio.

195   *Lollio.* I'll make him understand it easily. Cousin,
stand there.

    Antonio. Ay, cousin.

    Lollio. Master, stand you next the fool.

    Alibius. Well, Lollio?

200   *Lollio.* Here's my place. Mark now, Tony, there's a
fool before a knave.

    Antonio. That's I, cousin.

    Lollio. Here's a fool behind a knave, that's I; and
between us two fools there is a knave, that's my master;

205 'tis but we three, that's all.

    Antonio. We three, we three, cousin.

                        Madmen within.

    1 Madman within. Put's head i' th' pillory, the
bread's too little.

    2 Madman within. Fly, fly, and he catches the swallow.

200 *there's* ed. (there *Q*)

3 Madman within. Give her more onion, or the devil   210
     put the rope about her crag.

Lollio. You may hear what time of day it is, the chimes
     of Bedlam goes.

Alibius. Peace, peace, or the wire comes!

3 Madman within. Cat whore, cat whore, her par-   215
     masant, her parmasant!

Alibius. Peace, I say!—Their hour's come, they must
     be fed, Lollio.

Lollio. There's no hope of recovery of that Welsh
madman, was undone by a mouse that spoiled him a   220
parmasant; lost his wits for't.

Alibius. Go to your charge, Lollio, I'll to mine.

Lollio. Go you to your madmen's ward, let me alone
     with your fools.

Alibius. And remember my last charge, Lollio.   *Exit.*   225

Lollio. Of which your patients do you think I am?
Come, Tony, you must amongst your school-fellows
now; there's pretty scholars amongst 'em, I can tell
you, there's some of 'em at *stultus, stulta, stultum.*

Antonio. I would see the madmen, cousin, if they   230
     would not bite me.

Lollio. No, they shall not bite thee, Tony.

Antonio. They bite when they are at dinner, do they
not, coz?

Lollio. They bite at dinner, indeed, Tony. Well, I   235
hope to get credit by thee; I like thee the best of all the
scholars that ever I brought up, and thou shalt prove a
wise man, or I'll prove a fool myself.   *Exeunt.*

---

211 *crag* neck   214 *wire* whip
216 *parmasant* parmesan cheese
219-220 Proverbial fondness of Welsh for cheese

Act II, Scene i

Enter BEATRICE *and* JASPERINO *severally.*

Beatrice. Oh, sir, I'm ready now for that fair service
Which makes the name of friend sit glorious on you.
Good angels and this conduct be your guide;
                              [*Gives a paper.*]
Fitness of time and place is there set down, sir.

5   *Jasperino.* The joy I shall return rewards my service.
                                                    Exit.

Beatrice. How wise is Alsemero in his friend!
It is a sign he makes his choice with judgment.
Then I appear in nothing more approv'd
Than making choice of him;

10   For 'tis a principle, he that can choose
That bosom well, who of his thoughts partakes,
Proves most discreet in every choice he makes.
Methinks I love now with the eyes of judgment,
And see the way to merit, clearly see it.

15   A true deserver like a diamond sparkles,
In darkness you may see him, that's in absence,
Which is the greatest darkness falls in love;
Yet is he best discern'd then
With intellectual eyesight. What's Piracquo

20   My father spends his breath for? And his blessing
Is only mine as I regard his name,
Else it goes from me, and turns head against me,
Transform'd into a curse; some speedy way
Must be remember'd; he's so forward too,

25   So urgent that way, scarce allows me breath
To speak to my new comforts.

Scene, as for all the main plot, the Castle.

Enter DE FLORES.

De Flores [*aside*].   Yonder's she.
Whatever ails me, now a-late especially,
I can as well be hang'd as refrain seeing her;
Some twenty times a day, nay, not so little,
Do I force errands, frame ways and excuses   30
To come into her sight, and I have small reason for't,
And less encouragement; for she baits me still
Every time worse than other, does profess herself
The cruellest enemy to my face in town,
At no hand can abide the sight of me,   35
As if danger or ill luck hung in my looks.
I must confess my face is bad enough,
But I know far worse has better fortune,
And not endur'd alone, but doted on;
And yet such pick-hair'd faces, chins like witches',   40
Here and there five hairs, whispering in a corner,
As if they grew in fear one of another,
Wrinkles like troughs, where swine-deformity swills
The tears of perjury that lie there like wash
Fallen from the slimy and dishonest eye;   45
Yet such a one plucks sweets without restraint,
And has the grace of beauty to his sweet.
Though my hard fate has thrust me out to servitude,
I tumbled into th' world a gentleman.
She turns her blessed eye upon me now,   50
And I'll endure all storms before I part with't.
    Beatrice [*aside*]. Again!
—This ominous ill-fac'd fellow more disturbs me
Than all my other passions.
    De Flores [*aside*].   Now't begins again;
I'll stand this storm of hail though the stones pelt me.   55

40 *pick-hair'd* sparsely bearded   46 *plucks* ed. (pluckt *Q*)
47 *to his sweet* for his sweetheart

Beatrice. Thy business? What's thy business?

De Flores [*aside*].   Soft and fair,
I cannot part so soon now.

Beatrice [*aside*].   The villain's fix'd—

* Thou standing toad-pool!

De Flores [*aside*].   The shower falls amain now.

Beatrice. Who sent thee? What's thy errand? Leave
   my sight.

60 *De Flores.* My lord your father charg'd me to deliver
A message to you.

Beatrice.   What, another since?
Do't and be hang'd then, let me be rid of thee.

De Flores. True service merits mercy.

Beatrice.   What's thy message?

De Flores. Let beauty settle but in patience,
You shall hear all.

65 *Beatrice.*   A dallying, trifling torment!

De Flores. Signor Alonzo de Piracquo, lady,
Sole brother to Tomazo de Piracquo—

Beatrice. Slave, when wilt make an end?

De Flores.   Too soon I shall.

Beatrice. What all this while of him?

De Flores.   The said Alonzo,
With the foresaid Tomazo—

70 *Beatrice.*   Yet again?

De Flores. Is new alighted.

Beatrice.   Vengeance strike the news!
Thou thing most loath'd, what cause was there in this
To bring thee to my sight?

De Flores.   My lord your father
Charg'd me to seek you out.

Beatrice.   Is there no other
To send his errand by?

75 *De Flores.*   It seems 'tis my luck

58 *standing* stagnant

To be i' th' way still.

    Beatrice.   Get thee from me.

    De Flores [*aside*].   So!

Why, am not I an ass to devise ways

Thus to be rail'd at? I must see her still!

I shall have a mad qualm within this hour again,

I know't, and, like a common Garden-bull,   80

I do but take breath to be lugg'd again.

What this may bode I know not; I'll despair the less,

Because there's daily precedents of bad faces

Belov'd beyond all reason; these foul chops

May come into favour one day 'mongst his fellows;   85

Wrangling has prov'd the mistress of good pastime;

As children cry themselves asleep, I ha' seen

Women have chid themselves abed to men.

                              Exit DE FLORES.

    Beatrice. I never see this fellow, but I think

Of some harm towards me, danger's in my mind still;   90

I scarce leave trembling of an hour after.

The next good mood I find my father in,

I'll get him quite discarded. Oh, I was

Lost in this small disturbance, and forgot

Affliction's fiercer torrent that now comes   95

To bear down all my comforts.

      Enter VERMANDERO, ALONZO, TOMAZO.

    Vermandero.   Y'are both welcome,

But an especial one belongs to you, sir,

To whose most noble name our love presents

The addition of a son, our son Alonzo.

    Alonzo. The treasury of honour cannot bring forth   100

A title I should more rejoice in, sir.

---

80 *common Garden-bull* Paris garden, on the Bankside, where bulls
    were baited
99 *addition* title

    Vermandero. You have improv'd it well; daughter,
        prepare,
The day will steal upon thee suddenly.
    Beatrice [*aside*]. Howe'er, I will be sure to keep the
        night,
If it should come so near me.

            [BEATRICE *and* VERMANDERO *talk apart.*]

    Tomazo.   Alonzo.
105   *Alonzo.*   Brother?
    Tomazo. In troth I see small welcome in her eye.
    Alonzo. Fie, you are too severe a censurer
Of love in all points, there's no bringing on you;
If lovers should mark everything a fault,
110 Affection would be like an ill-set book,
Whose faults might prove as big as half the volume.
    Beatrice. That's all I do entreat.
    Vermandero.   It is but reasonable,
I'll see what my son says to't: son Alonzo,
Here's a motion made but to reprieve
115 A maidenhead three days longer; the request
Is not far out of reason, for indeed
The former time is pinching.
    Alonzo.   Though my joys
Be set back so much time as I could wish
They had been forward, yet since she desires it,
120 The time is set as pleasing as before,
I find no gladness wanting.
    Vermandero.   May I ever
Meet it in that point still! Y'are nobly welcome, sirs.

           Exeunt VERMANDERO *and* BEATRICE.

    Tomazo. So: did you mark the dulnesss of her parting
        now?
    Alonzo. What dulness? Thou art so exceptious still!

104 *keep* be prepared against

Tomazo. Why, let it go then, I am but a fool   125
To mark your harms so heedfully.
    Alonzo.   Where's the oversight?
    Tomazo. Come, your faith's cozen'd in her, strongly
        cozen'd;
Unsettle your affection with all speed
Wisdom can bring it to, your peace is ruin'd else.
Think what a torment 'tis to marry one   130
Whose heart is leap'd into another's bosom;
If ever pleasure she receive from thee,
It comes not in thy name, or of thy gift;
She lies but with another in thine arms,
He the half-father unto all thy children   135
In the conception; if he get 'em not,
She helps to get 'em for him, and how dangerous
And shameful her restraint may go in time to,
It is not to be thought on without sufferings.
    Alonzo. You speak as if she lov'd some other,
    then.   140
    Tomazo. Do you apprehend so slowly?
    Alonzo.   Nay, and that
Be your fear only, I am safe enough.
Preserve your friendship and your counsel, brother,
For times of more distress; I should depart
An enemy, a dangerous, deadly one,   145
To any but thyself, that should but think
She knew the meaning of inconstancy,
Much less the use and practice; yet w'are friends;
Pray, let no more be urg'd; I can endure
Much, till I meet an injury to her,   150
Then I am not myself. Farewell, sweet brother;
How much w'are bound to heaven to depart lovingly.
                        Exit.

137 *him, and* ed. (him, in his passions, and *Q*).
137–8 *how dangerous ... to* what terrible effects restraint will
    have on her.

Tomazo. Why, here is love's tame madness; thus a
    man
Quickly steals into his vexation.

                     Exit.

Act II, Scene ii

Enter DIAPHANTA *and* ALSEMERO.

Diaphanta. The place is my charge, you have kept
    your hour,
And the reward of a just meeting bless you.
I hear my lady coming; complete gentleman,
I dare not be too busy with my praises,
Th'are dangerous things to deal with.   *Exit.*

5   *Alsemero.*   This goes well;
These women are the ladies' cabinets,
Things of most precious trust are lock'd into 'em.

Enter BEATRICE.

Beatrice. I have within mine eye all my desires;
Requests that holy prayers ascend heaven for,

10   And bring 'em down to furnish our defects,
Come not more sweet to our necessities
Than thou unto my wishes.
    Alsemero.   W'are so like
In our expressions, lady, that unless I borrow
The same words, I shall never find their equals.
    Beatrice. How happy were this meeting, this em-

15   brace,
If it were free from envy! This poor kiss,
It has an enemy, a hateful one,
That wishes poison to't; how well were I now

10 *bring* ed. (brings *Q*) *furnish our defects* make good our deficiencies
16 *envy* malice

If there were none such name known as Piracquo,
Nor no such tie as the command of parents!   20
I should be but too much blessed.

    Alsemero.   One good service
Would strike off both your fears, and I'll go near it too,
Since you are so distress'd; remove the cause,
The command ceases, so there's two fears blown out
With one and the same blast.

    Beatrice   Pray, let me find you, sir.   25
What might that service be so strangely happy?

    Alsemero. The honourablest piece 'bout man, valour.
I'll send a challenge to Piracquo instantly.

    Beatrice. How? Call you that extinguishing of fear,
When 'tis the only way to keep it flaming?   30
Are not you ventured in the action,
That's all my joys and comforts? Pray, no more, sir.
Say you prevail'd, y'are danger's and not mine then;
The law would claim you from me, or obscurity
Be made the grave to bury you alive.   35
I'm glad these thoughts come forth; oh, keep not one
Of this condition, sir; here was a course
Found to bring sorrow on her way to death;
The tears would ne'er ha' dried till dust had chok'd 'em.
Blood-guiltiness becomes a fouler visage,   40
[*aside*].—And now I think on one. I was to blame,
I ha' marr'd so good a market with my scorn;
'T had been done questionless; the ugliest creature   *
Creation fram'd for some use, yet to see
I could not mark so much where it should be!   45

    Alsemero. Lady,—

    Beatrice [*aside*]. Why, men of art make much of
      poison,
Keep one to expel another; where was my art?

    Alsemero. Lady, you hear not me.

33 *y'are* ed. (your *Q*)

Beatrice.   I do especially, sir;
The present times are not so sure of our side

50   As those hereafter may be; we must use 'em then
As thrifty folks their wealth, sparingly now,
Till the time opens.
  Alsemero.   You teach wisdom, lady.
  Beatrice. Within there! Diaphanta!

Enter DIAPHANTA.

  Diaphanta.   Do you call, madam?
  Beatrice. Perfect your service, and conduct this
        gentleman
The private way you brought him.

55   *Diaphanta.*   I shall, madam.
  Alsemero. My love's as firm as love e'er built upon.
                         Exeunt DIAPHANTA *and* ALSEMERO.

Enter DE FLORES.

  De Flores [*aside*]. I have watch'd this meeting, and do
        wonder much
What shall become of t'other; I'm sure both
Cannot be serv'd unless she transgress; happily

60   Then I'll put in for one; for if a woman
Fly from one point, from him she makes a husband,
She spreads and mounts then like arithmetic,
One, ten, a hundred, a thousand, ten thousand,
Proves in time sutler to an army royal.

65   Now do I look to be most richly rail'd at,
Yet I must see her.
  Beatrice [*aside*]. Why, put case I loath'd him
As much as youth and beauty hates a sepulchre,
Must I needs show it? Cannot I keep that secret,
And serve my turn upon him?—See, he's here.
—De Flores!

59 *happily* haply   64 *sutler* supplier

De Flores [*aside*]. Ha, I shall run mad with joy!   70
She call'd me fairly by my name, De Flores,
And neither rogue nor rascal.
    Beatrice.   What ha' you done
To your face a-late? Y'have met with some good physi-
      cian;
Y'have prun'd yourself, methinks; you were not wont   ✽
To look so amorously.
    De Flores [*aside*].   Not I;   75
'Tis the same physnomy, to a hair and pimple,
Which she call'd scurvy scarce an hour ago;
How is this?
    Beatrice. Come hither; nearer, man.
    De Flores [*aside*]. I'm up to the chin in heaven!
    Beatrice.   Turn, let me see;
Faugh, 'tis but the heat of the liver, I perceiv't;   80
I thought it had been worse.
    De Flores [*aside*].   Her fingers touch'd me!
She smells all amber.
    Beatrice. I'll make a water for you shall cleanse this
Within a fortnight.
    De Flores.   With your own hands, lady?
    Beatrice. Yes, mine own, sir; in a work of cure   85
I'll trust no other.
    De Flores [*aside*]. 'Tis half an act of pleasure
To hear her talk thus to me.
    Beatrice.   When w'are us'd
To a hard face, 'tis not so unpleasing;
It mends still in opinion, hourly mends,
I see it by experience.
    De Flores [*aside*].   I was blest   90
To light upon this minute; I'll make use on't.
    Beatrice. Hardness becomes the visage of a man well,

74 *prun'd* preened, adorned   75 *amorously* fit to be loved
82 *amber* of ambergris, perfumed

It argues service, resolution, manhood,
If cause were of employment.

    De Flores.   'Twould be soon seen,
95 If e'er your ladyship had cause to use it.
I would but wish the honour of a service
So happy as that mounts to.

    Beatrice.   We shall try you—
Oh my De Flores!

    De Flores [*aside*]. How's that? She calls me hers
Already, *my* De Flores!—You were about
To sigh out somewhat, madam?

100   *Beatrice.*   No, was I?
I forgot—Oh!—

    De Flores.   There 'tis again, the very fellow on't.
    Beatrice. You are too quick, sir.
    De Flores. There's no excuse for't now; I heard it
        twice, madam;
That sigh would fain have utterance, take pity on't,
105 And lend it a free word; 'las, how it labours
For liberty! I hear the murmur yet
Beat at your bosom.

    Beatrice.   Would creation—
    De Flores. Ay, well said, that's it.
    Beatrice.   Had form'd me man!
    De Flores. Nay, that's not it.
    Beatrice.   Oh, 'tis the soul of freedom!
110 I should not then be forc'd to marry one
I hate beyond all depths; I should have power
Then to oppose my loathings, nay, remove 'em
For ever from my sight.

    De Flores [*aside*].   O blest occasion!—
Without change to your sex, you have your wishes.
Claim so much man in me.

115   *Beatrice.*   In thee, De Flores?
There's small cause for that.

De Flores.   Put it not from me;
It's a service that I kneel for to you.   [*Kneels.*]
     Beatrice. You are too violent to mean faithfully;
There's horror in my service, blood and danger;
Can those be things to sue for?
     De Flores.   If you knew   120
How sweet it were to me to be employed
In any act of yours, you would say then
I fail'd, and us'd not reverence enough
When I receive the charge on't.
     Beatrice [*aside*].   This is much, methinks;
Belike his wants are greedy, and to such   125
Gold tastes like angel's food.—Rise.
     De Flores. I'll have the work first.
     Beatrice [*aside*].   Possible his need
Is strong upon him.—There's to encourage thee;
                    [*Gives him money.*]
As thou art forward and thy service dangerous,
Thy reward shall be precious.
     De Flores.   That I have thought on;   130
I have assur'd myself of that beforehand,
And know it will be precious; the thought ravishes.
     Beatrice. Then take him to thy fury!
     De Flores.   I thirst for him.
     Beatrice. Alonzo de Piracquo!
     De Flores.   His end's upon him;
He shall be seen no more.
     Beatrice.   How lovely now   135
Dost thou appear to me! Never was man
Dearlier rewarded.
     De Flores.   I do think of that.
     Beatrice. Be wondrous careful in the execution.
     De Flores. Why, are not both our lives upon the cast?
     Beatrice. Then I throw all my fears upon thy service.   140
     De Flores. They ne'er shall rise to hurt you.

Beatrice.   When the deed's done,
I'll furnish thee with all things for thy flight;
Thou may'st live bravely in another country.
    De Flores. Ay, ay, we'll talk of that hereafter.
    Beatrice [aside].   I shall rid myself
145 Of two inveterate loathings at one time,
Piracquo, and his dog-face.

                                              Exit.

*   *De Flores.*   Oh my blood!
Methinks I feel her in mine arms already,
Her wanton fingers combing out this beard,
And, being pleased, praising this bad face.
150 Hunger and pleasure, they'll commend sometimes
Slovenly dishes, and feed heartily on 'em,
Nay, which is stranger, refuse daintier for 'em.
Some women are odd feeders.—I'm too loud.
Here comes the man goes supperless to bed,
155 Yet shall not rise tomorrow to his dinner.

                    Enter ALONZO.

    Alonzo. De Flores.
    De Flores.   My kind, honourable lord?
    Alonzo. I am glad I ha' met with thee.
    De Flores.   Sir?
    Alonzo.   Thou canst show me
The full strength of the castle?
    De Flores.   That I can, sir.
    Alonzo. I much desire it.
    De Flores.   And if the ways and straits
160 Of some of the passages be not too tedious for you,
I will assure you, worth your time and sight, my lord.
*   *Alonzo.* Push, that shall be no hindrance.
    De Flores.   I'm your servant then.

146 *blood* lust, sensual desire

'Tis now near dinner time; 'gainst your lordship's rising
I'll have the keys about me.
   Alonzo.   Thanks, kind De Flores.
   De Flores [*aside*]. He's safely thrust upon me beyond
      hopes.   165
                                        Exeunt.

Act III, Scene i

Enter ALONZO *and* DE FLORES.

(*In the act-time* DE FLORES *hides a naked rapier.*)

   De Flores. Yes, here are all the keys; I was afraid, my
      lord,
I'd wanted for the postern, this is it.
I've all, I've all, my lord; this for the sconce.
   Alonzo. 'Tis a most spacious and impregnable fort.
   De Flores. You'll tell me more, my lord: this descent   5
Is somewhat narrow, we shall never pass
Well with our weapons, they'll but trouble us.
   Alonzo. Thou say'st true.
   De Flores.   Pray let me help your lordship.
   Alonzo. 'Tis done. Thanks, kind De Flores.
   De Flores.   Here are hooks, my lord,
To hang such things on purpose.
                              [*He hangs up the swords.*]
   Alonzo.   Lead, I'll follow thee.   10
                Exeunt at one door and enter at the other.

act-time interval between acts
   3 *sconce* small fort or earth work
   8 Alonzo and De Flores remove their swords, before entering
      the vaults

Act III, Scene ii

De Flores. All this is nothing; you shall see anon
A place you little dream on.
   Alonzo.   I am glad
I have this leisure; all your master's house
Imagine I ha' taken a gondola.
   De Flores. All but myself, sir,—[*aside*] which makes
5   up my safety.
My lord, I'll place you at a casement here
Will show you the full strength of all the castle.
Look, spend your eye awhile upon that object.
   Alonzo. Here's rich variety, De Flores.
   De Flores.   Yes, sir.
   Alonzo. Goodly munition.
10   *De Flores.*   Ay, there's ordnance, sir,
No bastard metal, will ring you a peal like bells
At great men's funerals; keep your eye straight, my lord;
Take special notice of that sconce before you,
There you may dwell awhile.   [*Takes up the rapier.*]
   Alonzo.   I am upon't.
   De Flores. And so am I.

                       [*Stabs him.*]
15   *Alonzo.*   De Flores! Oh, De Flores!
Whose malice hast thou put on?
   De Flores.   Do you question
A work of secrecy? I must silence you.   [*Stabs him.*]
   Alonzo. Oh, oh, oh!
   De Flores.   I must silence you. [*Stabs him.*]
So here's an undertaking well accomplish'd.
20   This vault serves to good use now.—Ha, what's that
Threw sparkles in my eye? Oh, 'tis a diamond

He wears upon his finger; it was well found,
This will approve the work. What, so fast on?
Not part in death? I'll take a speedy course then,
Finger and all shall off [*Cuts off the finger*]. So now I'll
    clear 25
The passages from all suspect or fear.

                    Exit with body.

Act III, Scene iii

Enter ISABELLA *and* LOLLIO.

Isabella. Why, sirrah? Whence have you commission
To fetter the doors against me? If you
Keep me in a cage, pray whistle to me,
Let me be doing something.
    Lollio. You shall be doing, if it please you; I'll whistle * 5
to you if you'll pipe after.
    Isabella. Is it your master's pleasure or your own,
To keep me in this pinfold?
    Lollio. 'Tis for my master's pleasure, lest being taken
in another man's corn, you might be pounded in 10
another place.
    Isabella. 'Tis very well, and he'll prove very wise.
    Lollio. He says you have company enough in the
house, if you please to be sociable, of all sorts of people.
    Isabella. Of all sorts? Why, here's none but fools and 15
    madmen.
    Lollio. Very well; and where will you find any other,
if you should go abroad? There's my master and I to
boot too.
    Isabella. Of either sort one, a madman and a fool.

23 *approve* confirm
 8 *pinfold* pen, pound

R—C

20   *Lollio.* I would even participate of both then, if I
were as you; I know y'are half mad already, be half
foolish too.

Isabella. Y'are a brave, saucy rascal! Come on, sir,
Afford me then the pleasure of your bedlam;
25   You were commending once today to me
Your last-come lunatic; what a proper
Body there was without brains to guide it,
And what a pitiful delight appear'd
In that defect, as if your wisdom had found
30   A mirth in madness; pray, sir, let me partake,
If there be such a pleasure.

Lollio. If I do not show you the handsomest, dis-
creetest madman, one that I may call the understanding
madman, then say I am a fool.

35   *Isabella.* Well, a match, I will say so.

Lollio. When you have a taste of the madman, you
shall, if you please, see Fools' College, o' th' side; I seldom lock there, 'tis but shooting a bolt or two, and you
are amongst 'em.

Exit. Enter presently.

40   Come on, sir, let me see how handsomely you'll behave
yourself now.

Enter FRANCISCUS.

Franciscus. How sweetly she looks! Oh, but there's a
wrinkle in her brow as deep as philosophy. Anacreon,
drink to my mistress' health, I'll pledge it; stay, stay,
45 *   there's a spider in the cup! no, 'tis but a grape-stone;
swallow it, fear nothing, poet; so, so, lift higher.

Isabella. Alack, alack, 'tis too full of pity
To be laugh'd at. How fell he mad? Canst thou tell?

Lollio. For love, mistress; he was a pretty poet too,

43 *Anacreon* Greek poet, said to have choked to death on grape-
      stone, while drinking wine
45 *spider* considered poisonous

and that set him forwards first; the Muses then forsook   50
him; he ran mad for a chambermaid, yet she was but a
dwarf neither.

Franciscus. Hail, bright Titania!
Why stand'st thou idle on these flow'ry banks?
Oberon is dancing with his Dryades;   55
I'll gather daisies, primrose, violets,
And bind them in a verse of poesie.

Lollio. Not too near; you see your danger.
                                        [*Shows the whip.*]

Franciscus. Oh, hold thy hand, great Diomed!
Thou feed'st thy horses well, they shall obey thee;   60
Get up, Bucephalus kneels.
                                        [*Kneels.*]

Lollio. You see how I awe my flock; a shepherd has
not his dog at more obedience.

Isabella. His conscience is unquiet; sure that was
The cause of this. A proper gentleman.   65

Franciscus. Come hither, Esculapius; hide the poison.

Lollio. Well, 'tis hid.   [*Hides the whip.*]

Franciscus. Didst thou never hear of one Tiresias,
A famous poet?

Lollio. Yes, that kept tame wild geese.   70

Franciscus. That's he; I am the man.

Lollio. No!

Franciscus. Yes, but make no words on't; I was a man
Seven years ago.

Lollio. A stripling I think you might.   *   75

Franciscus. Now I'm a woman, all feminine.

Lollio. I would I might see that.

Franciscus. Juno struck me blind.

Lollio. I'll ne'er believe that; for a woman, they say,

---

59 *Diomed* Diomedes, Thracian king, who fed human flesh to
   horses
66 *Esculapius* Greek god of healing
68 *Tiresias* Theban soothsayer who changed his sex

80   has an eye more than a man.

    Franciscus. I say she struck me blind.

    Lollio. And Luna made you mad; you have two trades to beg with.

    Franciscus. Luna is now big-bellied, and there's room

85   For both of us to ride with Hecate;

    I'll drag thee up into her silver sphere,

    And there we'll kick the dog, and beat the bush,

    That barks against the witches of the night,

*   The swift lycanthropi that walks the round,

90   We'll tear their wolvish skins and save the sheep.

                  [*Tries to seize* LOLLIO.]

    Lollio. Is't come to this? Nay, then my poison comes forth again [*shows the whip*]; mad slave, indeed, abuse your keeper!

    Isabella. I prithee, hence with him, now he grows
        dangerous.

95   *Franciscus* (*sings*). *Sweet love, pity me.*

    Give me leave to lie with thee.

    Lollio. No, I'll see you wiser first; to your own kennel.

    Franciscus. No noise, she sleeps, draw all the curtains
        round,

    Let no soft sound molest the pretty soul,

100   But love, and love creeps in at a mouse-hole.

    Lollio. I would you would get into your hole!

                     Exit FRANCISCUS.

Now, mistress, I will bring you another sort, you shall be fooled another while; Tony, come hither, Tony; look who's yonder, Tony.

Enter ANTONIO.

105   *Antonio*. Cousin, is it not my aunt?

82–83 *two trades* blindness and madness

    85 *Hecate* Goddess of witchcraft; here, as frequently, the moon

    87 *dog . . . bush* possessions of the man in the moon

    89 *lycanthropi* those in grip of wolf-madness

    105 *aunt* prostitute

Lollio. Yes, 'tis one of 'em, Tony.

Antonio. He, he! How do you, uncle?

Lollio. Fear him not, mistress, 'tis a gentle nigget; you may play with him, as safely with him as with his bauble.   110

Isabella. How long hast thou been a fool?

Antonio. Ever since I came hither, cousin.

Isabella. Cousin? I'm none of thy cousins, fool.

Lollio. Oh mistress, fools have always so much wit as
  to claim their kindred.   115

Madman within. Bounce, bounce, he falls, he falls!

Isabella. Hark you, your scholars in the upper room
Are out of order.

Lollio. Must I come amongst you there? Keep you
the fool, mistress; I'll go up and play left-handed   120
Orlando amongst the madmen.   *Exit.*

Isabella. Well, sir.

Antonio. 'Tis opportuneful now, sweet lady! Nay,
Cast no amazing eye upon this change.

Isabella. Ha!   125

Antonio. This shape of folly shrouds your dearest
  love,
The truest servant to your powerful beauties,
Whose magic had this force thus to transform me.

Isabella. You are a fine fool indeed.

Antonio.   Oh, 'tis not strange;
Love has an intellect that runs through all   130
The scrutinous sciences, and, like
A cunning poet catches a quantity
Of every knowledge, yet brings all home
Into one mystery, into one secret
That he proceeds in.

Isabella.   Y'are a parlous fool.   135

108 *nigget* fool
110 *bauble* fool's stick; often sexual innuendo
121 *Orlando* Ariosto's *Orlando Furioso*

Antonio. No danger in me; I bring naught but love
And his soft-wounding shafts to strike you with.
Try but one arrow; if it hurt you,
I'll stand you twenty back in recompense.

[*Kisses her.*]

Isabella. A forward fool too!

140 *Antonio.*   This was love's teaching
A thousand ways he fashion'd out my way,
And this I found the safest and the nearest
To tread the Galaxia to my star.

Isabella. Profound, withal! Certain, you dream'd of
this;
Love never taught it waking.

145 *Antonio.*   Take no acquaintance
Of these outward follies; there is within
A gentleman that loves you.

Isabella.   When I see him,
I'll speak with him; so in the meantime keep
Your habit, it becomes you well enough.

150 As you are a gentleman, I'll not discover you;
That's all the favour that you must expect;
When you are weary, you may leave the school,
For all this while you have but play'd the fool.

Enter LOLLIO.

Antonio. And must again.—He, he! I thank you,
cousin;

155 I'll be your valentine tomorrow morning.

Lollio. How do you like the fool, mistress?

Isabella. Passing well, sir.

Lollio. Is he not witty, pretty well for a fool?

Isabella. If he hold on as he begins, he is like

160 To come to something.

Lollio. Ay, thank a good tutor; you may put him to't;

142 *the nearest* ed. (nearest *Q*)
143 *Galaxia* Milky Way

he begins to answer pretty hard questions. Tony, how
many is five times six?

Antonio. Five times six is six times five.

Lollio. What arithmetician could have answered   165
better? How many is one hundred and seven?

Antonio. One hundred and seven is seven hundred
and one, cousin.

Lollio. This is no wit to speak on; will you be rid of
the fool now?   170

Isabella. By no means, let him stay a little.

Madman within. Catch there, catch the last couple   *
in hell!

Lollio. Again! must I come amongst you? Would my
master were come home! I am not able to govern   175
both these wards together.   *Exit.*

Antonio. Why should a minute of love's hour be lost?

Isabella. Fie, out again! I had rather you kept
Your other posture; you become not your tongue
When you speak from your clothes.

Antonio.   How can he freeze,   180
Lives near so sweet a warmth? Shall I alone
Walk through the orchard of the Hesperides,
And cowardly not dare to pull an apple?
This with the red cheeks I must venture for.

    [*Tries to kiss her.*]

Enter LOLLIO *above.*

Isabella. Take heed, there's giants keep 'em.   185

Lollio [*aside*]. How now, fool, are you good at that?
Have you read Lipsius? He's past *Ars Amandi*; I believe
I must put harder questions to him, I perceive that.

Isabella. You are bold without fear too.

Antonio.   What should I fear,

180 *from your clothes* in fool's garb
187 *Lipsius* reference to scholar, solely for sake of pun
    Ars Amandi Ovid's handbook of love i.e. an old hand at love

190 Having all joys about me? Do you smile,
And love shall play the wanton on your lip,
Meet and retire, retire and meet again;
Look you but cheerfully, and in your eyes
I shall behold mine own deformity,
195 And dress myself up fairer; I know this shape
Becomes me not, but in those bright mirrors
I shall array me handsomely.

    Lollio.   Cuckoo, cuckoo!

                               Exit.

    [Enter] MADMEN *above, some as birds, other as beasts.*

    Antonio. What are these?

    Isabella.   Of fear enough to part us;
Yet they are but our schools of lunatics,
200 That act their fantasies in any shapes
Suiting their present thoughts; if sad, they cry;
If mirth be their conceit, they laugh again.
Sometimes they imitate the beasts and birds,
Singing, or howling, braying, barking; all
As their wild fancies prompt 'em.

             Enter LOLLIO.

205   *Antonio.*   These are no fears.

    Isabella. But here's a large one, my man.

    Antonio. Ha, he! That's fine sport indeed, cousin.

    Lollio. I would my master were come home, 'tis too
much for one shepherd to govern two of these flocks;
210 nor can I believe that one churchman can instruct two
benefices at once; there will be some incurable mad of
the one side, and very fools on the other. Come, Tony.

    Antonio. Prithee, cousin, let me stay here still.

    Lollio. No, you must to your book now, you have
215   played sufficiently.

    197 *cuckoo* a warning of cuckoldry pending

Isabella. Your fool is grown wondrous witty.

Lollio. Well, I'll say nothing; but I do not think but
　　he will put you down one of these days.

Exeunt LOLLIO *and* ANTONIO.

Isabella. Here the restrained current might make
　　breach,

Spite of the watchful bankers; would a woman stray,　　220
She need not gad abroad to seek her sin,
It would be brought home one ways or other:
The needle's point will to the fixed north;
Such drawing arctics women's beauties are.

Enter LOLLIO.

Lollio. How dost thou, sweet rogue?　　　　　　225

Isabella. How now?

Lollio. Come, there are degrees, one fool may be
better than another.

Isabella. What's the matter?

Lollio. Nay, if thou giv'st thy mind to fool's-flesh,　230
have at thee!

[*Tries to kiss her.*]

Isabella. You bold slave, you!

Lollio. I could follow now as t'other fool did:
'What should I fear,
Having all joys about me? Do you but smile,　　　235
And love shall play the wanton on your lip,
Meet and retire, retire and meet again;
Look you but cheerfully, and in your eyes
I shall behold my own deformity,
And dress myself up fairer; I know this shape　　240
Becomes me not,—'
and so as it follows, but is not this the more foolish way?
Come, sweet rogue; kiss me, my little Lacedemonian.

---

220 *bankers* dike-builders
243 *Lacedemonian* lit. a Spartan; of few words (?)

Let me feel how thy pulses beat; thou hast a thing about
245　thee would do a man pleasure, I'll lay my hand on't.
　　Isabella. Sirrah, no more! I see you have discovered
This love's knight-errant, who hath made adventure
For purchase of my love; be silent, mute,
Mute as a statue, or his injunction,
250　For me enjoying, shall be to cut thy throat;
I'll do it, though for no other purpose,
And be sure he'll not refuse it.
　　Lollio. My share, that's all; I'll have my fool's part
with you.
　　Isabella. No more! Your master.

Enter ALIBIUS.

255　*Alibius.*　　　　　　　　　　Sweet, how dost thou?
　　Isabella. Your bounden servant, sir.
　　Alibius.　　　　　　　　　　Fie, fie, sweetheart,
No more of that.
　　Isabella.　　You were best lock me up.
　　Alibius. In my arms and bosom, my sweet Isabella,
I'll lock thee up most nearly. Lollio,
260　We have employment, we have task in hand;
At noble Vermandero's, our castle captain,
There is a nuptial to be solemniz'd—
Beatrice-Joanna, his fair daughter, bride,—
For which the gentleman hath bespoke our pains,
265　A mixture of our madmen and our fools,
To finish, as it were, and make the fag
Of all the revels, the third night from the first;
Only an unexpected passage over,
To make a frightful pleasure, that is all,
270　But not the all I aim at; could we so act it,
To teach it in a wild, distracted measure;
Though out of form and figure, breaking time's head,

268 *unexpected passage* sudden appearance of madmen

It were no matter, 'twould be heal'd again
In one age or other, if not in this.
This, this, Lollio; there's a good reward begun,   275
And will beget a bounty be it known.

    Lollio. This is easy, sir, I'll warrant you; you have
about you fools and madmen that can dance very well,
and 'tis no wonder, your best dancers are not the wisest
men; the reason is, with often jumping they jolt their   280
brains down into their feet, that their wits lie more in
their heels than in their heads.

    Alibius. Honest Lollio, thou givest me a good reason
And a comfort in it.

    Isabella.   Y'have a fine trade on't,
Madmen and fools are a staple commodity.   285

    Alibius. Oh wife, we must eat, wear clothes, and live;
Just at the lawyer's haven we arrive,   *
By madmen and by fools we both do thrive.   *Exeunt.*

Act III, Scene iv

Enter VERMANDERO, ALSEMERO, JASPERINO, *and* BEATRICE

    Vermandero. Valencia speaks so nobly of you, sir,
I wish I had a daughter now for you.

    Alsemero. The fellow of this creature were a partner
For a king's love.

    Vermandero.   I had her fellow once, sir,
But Heaven has married her to joys eternal;   5
'Twere sin to wish her in this vale again.
Come, sir, your friend and you shall see the pleasures
Which my health chiefly joys in.

    Alsemero. I hear the beauty of this seat largely.   *

287 *lawyer's haven* wealth
  9 *largely* at length; over a large area

Vermandero. It falls much short of that.

Exeunt. Manet BEATRICE.

10   *Beatrice.*   So, here's one step
Into my father's favour; time will fix him.
I have got him now the liberty of the house;
So wisdom by degrees works out her freedom;
And if that eye be dark'ned that offends me—
15   I wait but that eclipse—this gentleman
Shall soon shine glorious in my father's liking,
Through the refulgent virtue of my love.

Enter DE FLORES.

*   *De Flores* [*aside*]. My thoughts are at a banquet; for
    the deed,
I feel no weight in't, 'tis but light and cheap
20   For the sweet recompense that I set down for't.
Beatrice. De Flores.
De Flores.   Lady?
Beatrice.   Thy looks promise cheerfully.
De Flores. All things are answerable, time, circum-
    stance,
Your wishes, and my service.
Beatrice.   Is it done then?
De Flores. Piracquo is no more.
Beatrice. My joys start at mine eyes; our sweet'st
25   delights
Are evermore born weeping.
De Flores.   I've a token for you.
Beatrice. For me?
De Flores.   But it was sent somewhat unwillingly,
I could not get the ring without the finger.

[*Shows her the finger.*]

Beatrice. Bless me! What hast thou done?

18 *banquet; . . . deed* ed. (banquet . . . deed *Q*)

De Flores.   Why, is that more
Than killing the whole man? I cut his heart-strings.   30
A greedy hand thrust in a dish at court
In a mistake hath had as much as this.

  Beatrice. 'Tis the first token my father made me send
      him.

  De Flores. And I [have] made him send it back again
For his last token; I was loath to leave it,   35
And I'm sure dead men have no use of jewels.
He was as loath to part with't, for it stuck
As if the flesh and it were both one substance.

  Beatrice. At the stag's fall the keeper has his fees;
'Tis soon applied, all dead men's fees are yours, sir.   40
I pray, bury the finger, but the stone
You may make use on shortly; the true value,
Take't of my truth, is near three hundred ducats.

  De Flores. 'Twill hardly buy a capcase for one's con-
      science, though,
To keep it from the worm, as fine as 'tis.   45
Well, being my fees, I'll take it;
Great men have taught me that, or else my merit
Would scorn the way on't.

  Beatrice.   It might justly, sir;
Why, thou mistak'st, De Flores, 'tis not given
In state of recompense.

  De Flores.   No, I hope so, lady,   50
You should soon witness my contempt to't then.

  Beatrice. Prithee, thou look'st as if thou wert offended.

  De Flores. That were strange, lady; 'tis not possible
My service should draw such a cause from you.
Offended? Could you think so? That were much   55
For one of my performance, and so warm
Yet in my service.

  44 *capcase* protective cover, (lit. travelling bag.)
  45 *worm* gnawing remorse

Beatrice. 'Twere misery in me to give you cause, sir.

De Flores. I know so much, it were so, misery
In her most sharp condition.

60   *Beatrice.*   'Tis resolv'd then;
Look you, sir, here's three thousand golden florins;
I have not meanly thought upon thy merit

De Flores. What, salary? Now you move me.

Beatrice.   How, De Flores?

De Flores. Do you place me in the rank of verminous fellows,

65 To destroy things for wages? Offer gold?
The life blood of man! Is anything
Valued too precious for my recompense?

Beatrice. I understand thee not.

De Flores.   I could ha' hir'd
A journeyman in murder at this rate,

70 And mine own conscience might have slept at ease,
And have had the work brought home.

Beatrice [*aside*].   I'm in a labyrinth;
What will content him? I would fain be rid of him.—
I'll double the sum, sir.

De Flores.   You take a course
To double my vexation, that's the good you do.

Beatrice [*aside*]. Bless me! I am now in worse plight
75   than I was;
I know not what will please him.—For my fear's sake,
I prithee make away with all speed possible
And if thou be'st so modest not to name
The sum that will content thee, paper blushes not;
80 Send thy demand in writing, it shall follow thee,
But prithee take thy flight.

---

70 *Slept at ease* ed. (*not in Q*). All editors accept Dilke's
addition to incomplete line.

De Flores.   You must fly too then.

Beatrice. I?

De Flores. I'll not stir a foot else.

Beatrice.   What's your meaning?

De Flores. Why, are not you as guilty, in, I'm sure,
As deep as I? And we should stick together.
Come, your fears counsel you but ill; my absence   85
Would draw suspect upon you instantly;
There were no rescue for you.

    Beatrice [*aside*].   He speaks home.

De Flores. Nor is it fit we two engag'd so jointly,
Should part and live asunder.

    Beatrice.   How now, sir?
This shows not well.

    De Flores.   What makes your lip so strange?   90
This must not be betwixt us.

    Beatrice [*aside*].   The man talks wildly.

De Flores. Come, kiss me with a zeal now.

    Beatrice [*aside*].   Heaven, I doubt him!

De Flores. I will not stand so long to beg 'em shortly.

Beatrice. Take heed, De Flores, of forgetfulness,
'Twill soon betray us.

    De Flores.   Take you heed first;   95
Faith, y'are grown much forgetful, y'are to blame in't.

    Beatrice [*aside*]. He's bold, and I am blam'd for't!

De Flores.   I have eas'd
You of your trouble, think on't, I'm in pain,
And must be eas'd of you; 'tis a charity,
Justice invites your blood to understand me.   100

    Beatrice. I dare not.

De Flores.   Quickly!

    Beatrice.   Oh, I never shall!
Speak it yet further off that I may lose
What has been spoken, and no sound remain on't.

90 *strange* unfriendly   92 *doubt* suspect, fear

I would not hear so much offence again
For such another deed.

105   *De Flores.*   Soft, lady, soft;
The last is not yet paid for. Oh, this act
Has put me into spirit; I was as greedy on't
As the parch'd earth of moisture, when the clouds weep.
Did you not mark, I wrought myself into't,
110 Nay, sued and kneel'd for't? Why was all that pains took?
You see I have thrown contempt upon your gold,
Not that I want it not, for I do piteously;
In order I will come unto't, and make use on't,
But 'twas not held so precious to begin with;
115 For I place wealth after the heels of pleasure,
And were I not resolv'd in my belief
That thy virginity were perfect in thee,
I should but take my recompense with grudging,
As if I had but half my hopes I agreed for.
120   *Beatrice.* Why, 'tis impossible thou canst be so wicked,
Or shelter such a cunning cruelty,
To make his death the murderer of my honour!
Thy language is so bold and vicious,
I cannot see which way I can forgive it
With any modesty.
125   *De Flores.* Push! You forget yourself!
A woman dipp'd in blood, and talk of modesty!
 Beatrice. Oh, misery of sin! Would I had been bound
Perpetually unto my living hate
In that Piracquo, than to hear these words.
130 Think but upon the distance that creation
Set 'twixt thy blood and mine, and keep thee there.
 De Flores. Look but into your conscience, read me
  there,
'Tis a true book, you'll find me there your equal.
Push! Fly not to your birth, but settle you

112 *it not* ed. (it *Q*)

In what the act has made you, y'are no more now.   135
You must forget your parentage to me:
Y'are the deed's creature; by that name
You lost your first condition, and I challenge you,
As peace and innocency has turn'd you out,
And made you one with me.

    Beatrice.   With thee, foul villain?   140
    De Flores. Yes, my fair murd'ress; do you urge me?
Though thou writ'st maid, thou whore in thy affection!
'Twas chang'd from thy first love, and that's a kind   *
Of whoredom in thy heart; and he's chang'd now,
To bring thy second on, thy Alsemero,   145
Whom (by all sweets that ever darkness tasted)
If I enjoy thee not, thou ne'er enjoy'st;
I'll blast the hopes and joys of marriage,
I'll confess all; my life I rate at nothing.

    Beatrice. De Flores!   150
    De Flores. I shall rest from all lovers' plagues then;
I live in pain now; that shooting eye
Will burn my heart to cinders.

    Beatrice.   Oh, sir, hear me.
    De Flores. She that in life and love refuses me,
In death and shame my partner she shall be.   155
    Beatrice [kneels]. Stay, hear me once for all; I make
       thee master
Of all the wealth I have in gold and jewels;
Let me go poor unto my bed with honour,
And I am rich in all things.

    De Flores.   Let this silence thee:
The wealth of all Valencia shall not buy   160
My pleasure from me;
Can you weep Fate from its determin'd purpose?
So soon may you weep me.

---

136 *to* in your dealings with   141 *urge* provoke
163 *may you* ed. (may weep *Q*)

Beatrice.   Vengeance begins;
Murder, I see, is followed by more sins.
165   Was my creation in the womb so curs'd,
It must engender with a viper first?
        De Flores. Come, rise, and shroud your blushes in my
            bosom;   [*Raises her.*]
Silence is one of pleasure's best receipts;
Thy peace is wrought for ever in this yielding.
170 *   'Las, how the turtle pants! Thou'lt love anon
What thou so fear'st and faint'st to venture on.
                                        Exeunt.

Act IV, Scene i
[*Dumb show.*]

Enter GENTLEMEN, VERMANDERO *meeting them
with action of wonderment at the flight of*
PIRACQUO. *Enter* ALSEMERO, *with* JASPERINO
and GALLANTS; VERMANDERO *points to him, the*
GENTLEMEN *seeming to applaud the choice.*
[*Exeunt*] ALSEMERO, JASPERINO, *and* GENTLE-
MEN; BEATRICE *the bride following in great state,
accompanied with* DIAPHANTA, ISABELLA, *and
other* GENTLEWOMEN; DE FLORES *after all, smil-
ing at the accident;* ALONZO'S *ghost appears to*
DE FLORES *in the midst of his smile, startles him,
showing him the hand whose finger he had cut
off. They pass over in great solemnity.*
                Enter BEATRICE.
Beatrice. This fellow has undone me endlessly,
Never was bride so fearfully distress'd;
The more I think upon th' ensuing night,
And whom I am to cope with in embraces,

170 *turtle* dove
s.d. *accident* incident

One who's ennobled both in blood and mind,   5
So clear in understanding,—that's my plague now—
Before whose judgment will my fault appear
Like malefactors' crimes before tribunals;
There is no hiding on't, the more I dive
Into my own distress; how a wise man   10
Stands for a great calamity! There's no venturing
Into his bed, what course soe'er I light upon,
Without my shame, which may grow up to danger;
He cannot but in justice strangle me
As I lie by him, as a cheater use me;   15
'Tis a precious craft to play with a false die
Before a cunning gamester. Here's his closet,
The key left in't, and he abroad i'th' park?
Sure 'twas forgot; I'll be so bold as look in't.

                              [*Opens closet.*]

Bless me! A right physician's closet 'tis,   20
Set round with vials, every one her mark too.
Sure he does practise physic for his own use,
Which may be safely call'd your great man's wisdom.
What manuscript lies here? 'The Book of Experiment,
Call'd Secrets in Nature'; so 'tis, 'tis so;   *   25
'How to know whether a woman be with child or no';
I hope I am not yet; if he should try though!
Let me see, folio forty-five. Here 'tis;
The leaf tuck'd down upon't, the place suspicious:
'If you would know whether a woman be with child or   30
not, give her two spoonfuls of the white water in
glass C'—
Where's that glass C? Oh, yonder, I see't now—
'and if she be with child she sleeps full twelve hours
after; if not, not.'   35

5 *who's* ed. (both *Q*)   11 *stands for* assures
23 *which . . . wisdom* by safeguarding him against poison
25 *Secrets in Nature: De Arcanis Naturae* by Antonius Mizaldus
   (1520–78)

None of that water comes into my belly.
I'll know you from a hundred; I could break you now,
Or turn you into milk, and so beguile
The master of the mystery, but I'll look to you.

40 Ha! That which is next is ten times worse:
'How to know whether a woman be a maid or not.'
If that should be apply'd, what would become of me?
Belike he has a strong faith of my purity,
That never yet made proof; but this he calls

45 'A merry sleight, but true experiment, the author
Antonius Mizaldus. Give the party you suspect the
quantity of a spoonful of the water in the glass M,
which, upon her that is a maid, makes three several
effects: 'twill make her incontinently gape, then fall into

50 a sudden sneezing, last into a violent laughing; else
dull, heavy, and lumpish.'
Where had I been?
I fear it, yet 'tis seven hours to bedtime.

Enter DIAPHANTA.

Diaphanta. Cuds, madam, are you here?
Beatrice [*aside*].   Seeing that wench now,
55 A trick comes in my mind; 'tis a nice piece
Gold cannot purchase.—I come hither, wench,
To look my lord.
    Diaphanta [*aside*]. Would I had such a cause
To look him too!—Why, he's i' th' park madam.
    Beatrice. There let him be.
*   *Diaphanta.*   Ay, madam, let him compass
60 Whole parks and forests, as great rangers do;
At roosting time a little lodge can hold 'em.
Earth-conquering Alexander, that thought the world
Too narrow for him, in the end had but his pit-hole.

52 *Where . . . been* what would have happened had I not seen this?
55 *nice piece* honest girl   57 *look* look for

Beatrice. I fear thou art not modest, Diaphanta.

Diaphanta. Your thoughts are so unwilling to be
    known, madam;   65

'Tis ever the bride's fashion towards bed time

To set light by her joys, as if she ow'd 'em not.

Beatrice. Her joys? Her fears, thou would'st say.

Diaphanta.   Fear of what?

Beatrice. Art thou a maid, and talk'st so to a maid?

You leave a blushing business behind,   70

Beshrew your heart for't!

Diaphanta.   Do you mean good sooth, madam?

Beatrice. Well, if I'd thought upon the fear at first,

Man should have been unknown.

Diaphanta.   Is't possible?

Beatrice. I will give a thousand ducats to that woman

Would try what my fear were, and tell me true   75

Tomorrow, when she gets from't; as she likes,

I might perhaps be drawn to't.

Diaphanta.   Are you in earnest?

Beatrice. Do you get the woman, then challenge me,

And see if I'll fly from't; but I must tell you

This by the way, she must be a true maid,   80

Else there's no trial, my fears are not hers else.

Diaphanta. Nay, she that I would put into your
    hands, madam,

Shall be a maid.

Beatrice.   You know I should be sham'd else,

Because she lies for me.

Diaphanta.   'Tis a strange humour;

But are you serious still? Would you resign   85

Your first night's pleasure, and give money too?

Beatrice. As willingly as live;—[*aside*] alas, the gold

Is but a by-bet to wedge in the honour.

Diaphanta. I do not know how the world goes abroad

88 *by-bet* additional lure

90 For faith or honesty, there's both requir'd in this.
Madam, what say you to me, and stray no further?
I've a good mind, in troth, to earn your money.
   Beatrice. Y'are too quick, I fear, to be a maid.
   Diaphanta. How? Not a maid? Nay, then you urge
     me, madam;
95 Your honourable self is not a truer
With all your fears upon you—
   Beatrice [*aside*].   Bad enough then.
   Diaphanta. Than I with all my lightsome joys about
     me.
   Beatrice. I'm glad to hear't then; you dare put your
     honesty
Upon an easy trial?
   Diaphanta.   Easy? Anything.
   Beatrice. I'll come to you straight. [*Goes to the closet.*]
100   *Diaphanta.* [*aside*]. She will not search me, will she,
Like the forewoman of a female jury?
   Beatrice. Glass M; ay, this is it; look, Diaphanta,
You take no worse than I do.   [*Drinks.*]
   Diaphanta.   And in so doing,
I will not question what 'tis, but take it.   [*Drinks.*]
105   *Beatrice* [*aside*]. Now if the experiment be true,
     'twill praise itself,
And give me noble ease:—Begins already;
                 [DIAPHANTA *gapes.*]
There's the first symptom; and what haste it makes
To fall into the second, there by this time!
               [DIAPHANTA *sneezes.*]
Most admirable secret! On the contrary,
110 It stirs not me a whit, which most concerns it.
   Diaphanta. Ha, ha, ha!
   Beatrice [*aside*]. Just in all things and in order,
As if 'twere circumscrib'd; one accident

112 *accident* symptom

Gives way unto another.

Diaphanta.   Ha, ha, ha!

Beatrice. How now, wench?

Diaphanta.   Ha, ha, ha! I am so, so light

At heart—ha, ha, ha!—so pleasurable.   115

But one swig more, sweet madam.

Beatrice.   Ay, tomorrow;

We shall have time to sit by't.

Diaphanta.   Now I'm sad again.

Beatrice. [*aside*] It lays itself so gently, too!—Come,
        wench,

Most honest Diaphanta I dare call thee now.

Diaphanta. Pray tell me, madam, what trick call you
        this?   120

Beatrice. I'll tell thee all hereafter; we must study

The carriage of this business.

Diaphanta.   I shall carry't well,

Because I love the burthen.

Beatrice.   About midnight

You must not fail to steal forth gently,

That I may use the place.

Diaphanta.   Oh, fear not, madam,   125

I shall be cool by that time;—the bride's place,

And with a thousand ducats! I'm for a justice now,

I bring a portion with me; I scorn small fools.

                                Exeunt.

Act IV, Scene ii

Enter VERMANDERO *and* SERVANT

Vermandero. I tell thee, knave, mine honour is in
        question,

A thing till now free from suspicion,
Nor ever was there cause; who of my gentlemen
Are absent? Tell me and truly how many and who.
5   *Servant.* Antonio, sir, and Franciscus.
Vermandero. When did they leave the castle?
Servant. Some ten days since, sir, the one intending
    to Briamata, th' other for Valencia.
Vermandero. The time accuses 'em; a charge of
    murder
10   Is brought within my castle gate, Piracquo's murder;
I dare not answer faithfully their absence;
A strict command of apprehension
Shall pursue 'em suddenly, and either wipe
The stain off clear, or openly discover it.
15   Provide me winged warrants for the purpose.

Exit servant.

See, I am set on again.

Enter TOMAZO.

Tomazo. I claim a brother of you.
Vermandero.   Y'are too hot,
Seek him not here.
Tomazo.   Yes, 'mongst your dearest bloods,
If my peace find no fairer satisfaction;
20   This is the place must yield account for him,
For here I left him, and the hasty tie
Of this snatch'd marriage gives strong testimony
Of his most certain ruin.
Vermandero.   Certain falsehood!
This is the place indeed; his breach of faith
25   Has too much marr'd both my abused love,
The honourable love I reserv'd for him,

---

8 *Briamata* another house of Vermandero's, 10 leagues away.
    (*Reynolds*)
11 *answer faithfully* account for, in good faith

And mock'd my daughter's joy; the prepar'd morning
Blush'd at his infidelity; he left
Contempt and scorn to throw upon those friends
Whose belief hurt 'em; oh, 'twas most ignoble 30
To take his flight so unexpectedly,
And throw such public wrongs on those that lov'd him.

   Tomazo. Then this is all your answer?

   Vermandero.   'Tis too fair
For one of his alliance; and I warn you
That this place no more see you. 35

                                          Exit.

Enter DE FLORES.

   Tomazo.   The best is,
There is more ground to meet a man's revenge on.—
Honest De Flores?

   De Flores.   That's my name indeed.
Saw you the bride? Good sweet sir, which way took she?

   Tomazo. I have bless'd mine eyes from seeing such a
     false one.

   De Flores [*aside*]. I'd fain get off, this man's not for
     my company, 40
I smell his brother's blood when I come near him.

   Tomazo. Come hither, kind and true one; I remember
My brother lov'd thee well.

   De Flores.   Oh, purely, dear sir!
[*aside*]—Methinks I am now again a-killing on him,
He brings it so fresh to me. 45

   Tomazo.   Thou canst guess, sirrah,—
One honest friend has an instinct of jealousy—
At some foul guilty person?

   De Flores.   'Las, sir,
I am so charitable I think none
Worse than myself.—You did not see the bride then?

   Tomazo. I prithee name her not. Is she not wicked? 50

*

    De Flores. No, no, a pretty, easy, round-pack'd sinner,
    As your most ladies are, else you might think
    I flatter'd her; but, sir, at no hand wicked,
    Till th' are so old their chins and noses meet,
55   And they salute witches. I am call'd, I think, sir.
    [*aside*].—His company ev'n o'erlays my conscience.

                              Exit.

    Tomazo. That De Flores has a wondrous honest
        heart;
    He'll bring it out in time, I'm assur'd on't.
    Oh, here's the glorious master of the day's joy;
60   'Twill not be long till he and I do reckon.

             Enter ALSEMERO.

    Sir!
    Alsemero. You are most welcome.
    Tomazo.   You may call that word back;
    I do not think I am, nor wish to be.
    Alsemero. 'Tis strange you found the way to this
        house then.
    Tomazo. Would I'd ne'er known the cause! I'm none
        of those, sir,
65   That come to give you joy and swill your wine;
    'Tis a more precious liquor that must lay
    The fiery thirst I bring.
    Alsemero.   Your words and you
    Appear to me great strangers.
    Tomazo.   Time and our swords
    May make us more acquainted; this the business:
70   I should have a brother in your place;
    How treachery and malice have dispos'd of him,
    I'm bound to inquire of him which holds his right,
    Which never could come fairly.

51 *round-pack'd* well-shaped. See note
54 *chins and noses* ed. (sins and vices *Q*) Dyce's emendation accept-
ed by all later eds.
60 *'Twill* ed. (I will *Q*)

 Alsemero.   You must look
To answer for that word, sir.
 Tomazo.   Fear you not,
I'll have it ready drawn at our next meeting. 75
Keep your day solemn. Farewell, I disturb it not;
I'll bear the smart with patience for a time.

            Exit.

 Alsemero. 'Tis somewhat ominous this, a quarrel
  enter'd
Upon this day; my innocence relieves me,

    Enter JASPERINO.

I should be wondrous sad else—Jasperino, 80
I have news to tell thee, strange news.
 Jasperino.   I ha' some too,
I think as strange as yours; would I might keep
Mine, so my faith and friendship might be kept in't!
Faith, sir, dispense a little with my zeal,
And let it cool in this.
 Alsemero.   This puts me on, 85
And blames thee for thy slowness.
 Jasperino.   All may prove nothing,
Only a friendly fear that leapt from me, sir.
 Alsemero. No question it may prove nothing; let's
  partake it, though.
 Jasperino. 'Twas Diaphanta's chance (for to that
  wench
I pretend honest love and she deserves it) 90
To leave me in a back part of the house,
A place we chose for private conference;
She was no sooner gone, but instantly
I heard your bride's voice in the next room to me;
And, lending more attention, found De Flores 95

76 *keep your day solemn* celebrate your wedding day
90 *pretend* offer

Louder than she.

Alsemero.   De Flores? Thou art out now.

Jasperino. You'll tell me more anon.

Alsemero.   Still I'll prevent thee;
The very sight of him is poison to her.

Jasperino. That made me stagger too, but Diaphanta
At her return confirm'd it.

100 *Alsemero.*   Diaphanta!

Jasperino. Then fell we both to listen, and words
        pass'd
Like those that challenge interest in a woman.

Alsemero. Peace! quench thy zeal; 'tis dangerous to
        thy bosom.

Jasperino. Then truth is full of peril.

Alsemero.   Such truths are.

105 —Oh, were she the sole glory of the earth,
Had eyes that could shoot fire into kings' breasts,
And touch'd, she sleeps not here! Yet I have time,
Though night be near, to be resolv'd hereof;
And, prithee, do not weigh me by my passions.

Jasperino. I never weigh'd friend so.

110 *Alsemero.*   Done charitably!
That key will lead thee to a pretty secret,
By a Chaldean taught me, and I have
My study upon some. Bring from my closet
A glass inscrib'd there with the letter M,
And question not my purpose.

115 *Jasperino.*   It shall be done, sir.

                                        Exit.

Alsemero. How can this hang together? Not an hour
        since,
Her woman came pleading her lady's fears,
Deliver'd her for the most timorous virgin

97 *prevent* forestall   107 *touch'd* corrupted
112 *have* ed. (I've *Q*)

That ever shrunk at man's name, and so modest,
She charg'd her weep out her request to me   120
That she might come obscurely to my bosom.

Enter BEATRICE.

Beatrice [*aside*]. All things go well; my woman's pre-
     paring yonder
For her sweet voyage, which grieves me to lose;
Necessity compels it; I lose all else.
Alsemero [*aside*]. Push! Modesty's shrine is set in
     yonder forehead,   125
I cannot be too sure though.—My Joanna!
Beatrice. Sir, I was bold to weep a message to you;
Pardon my modest fears.
Alsemero [*aside*].   The dove's not meeker;   *
She's abus'd, questionless.

Enter JASPERINO.

                    —Oh, are you come, sir?
Beatrice [*aside*]. The glass, upon my life! I see the
     letter.   130
Jasperino. Sir, this is M.
Alsemero.   'Tis it.
Beatrice [*aside*].   I am suspected.
Alsemero. How fitly our bride comes to partake with
     us!
Beatrice. What is't, my lord?
Alsemero.   No hurt.
Beatrice.   Sir, pardon me,
I seldom taste of any composition.
Alsemero. But this, upon my warrant, you shall ven-
     ture on.   135
Beatrice. I fear 'twill make me ill.
Alsemero.   Heaven forbid that!

121 *obscurely* in darkness
134 *composition* made-up drink

Beatrice [*aside*]. I'm put now to my cunning; th'
    effects I know,
If I can now but feign 'em handsomely.

                         [*Drinks.*]

Alsemero [*to* JASPERINO]. It has that secret virtue it
    ne'er miss'd, sir,
Upon a virgin.

140   *Jasperino.* Treble qualitied?

                [BEATRICE *gapes, then sneezes.*]

Alsemero. By all that's virtuous, it takes there,
    proceeds!

Jasperino. This is the strangest trick to know a maid
    by.

Beatrice. Ha, ha, ha!
You have given me joy of heart to drink, my lord.

145   *Alsemero.* No, thou hast given me such joy of heart,
That never can be blasted.

    Beatrice.   What's the matter, sir?

Alsemero [*to* JASPERINO]. See, now 'tis settled in a
    melancholy,
Keeps both the time and method.—My Joanna,
Chaste as the breath of heaven, or morning's womb,

150 That brings the day forth, thus my love encloses thee.

                         Exeunt.

Act IV, Scene iii

Enter ISABELLA *and* LOLLIO.

Isabella. O heaven! Is this the waning moon?
Does love turn fool, run mad, and all at once?
Sirrah, here's a madman, akin to the fool too,
A lunatic lover.

5   *Lollio.* No, no, not he I brought the letter from?

---

148 *keeps* ed. (keep *Q*)   1 *waning* ed. (waiting *Q*)
2 *all at* ed. (all *Q*)

Isabella. Compare his inside with his out, and tell me.

Lollio. The out's mad, I'm sure of that; I had a taste   *
on't. 'To the bright Andromeda, chief chambermaid to
the Knight of the Sun, at the sign of Scorpio, in the   *
middle region, sent by the bellows-mender of Aeolus.   10
Pay the post.' This is stark madness.

Isabella. Now mark the inside. [*Reads*]. 'Sweet lady,
having now cast off this counterfeit cover of a madman,
I appear to your best judgment a true and faithful lover
of your beauty.'   15

Lollio. He is mad still.

Isabella. 'If any fault you find, chide those perfections
in you which have made me imperfect; 'tis the same sun
that causeth to grow and enforceth to wither,—'

Lollio. Oh rogue!   20

Isabella. '—Shapes and transhapes, destroys and
builds again; I come in winter to you dismantled of my
proper ornaments; by the sweet splendour of your
cheerful smiles, I spring and live a lover.'

Lollio. Mad rascal still!   25

Isabella. 'Tread him not under foot, that shall appear
an honour to your bounties. I remain—mad till I speak
with you, from whom I expect my cure—Yours all, or
one beside himself, Franciscus.'

Lollio. You are like to have a fine time on't; my mas-   30
ter and I may give over our professions, I do not think
but you can cure fools and madmen faster than we,
with little pains too.

Isabella. Very likely.

Lollio. One thing I must tell you, mistress: you per-   35
ceive that I am privy to your skill; if I find you minister
once and set up the trade, I put in for my thirds, I shall
be mad or fool else.

6 *Inside . . . out* the address of the letter with the contents.
18 *have* ed. (have have *Q*)

Isabella. The first place is thine, believe it, Lollio,
40 If I do fall—

Lollio. I fall upon you.

Isabella. So.

Lollio. Well, I stand to my venture.

Isabella. But thy counsel now, how shall I deal with
'em?

45 *Lollio.* Why, do you mean to deal with 'em?

Isabella. Nay, the fair understanding, how to use 'em.

Lollio. Abuse 'em! That's the way to mad the fool,
and make a fool of the madman, and then you use 'em
kindly.

50 *Isabella.* 'Tis easy, I'll practise; do thou observe it;
The key of thy wardrobe.

Lollio. There; fit yourself for 'em, and I'll fit 'em both
for you.

[*Gives her the key.*]

Isabella. Take thou no further notice than the outside.

Exit.

55 *Lollio.* Not an inch; I'll put you to the inside.

Enter ALIBIUS.

Alibius. Lollio, art there? Will all be perfect, think'st
thou?

Tomorrow night, as if to close up the solemnity,
Vermandero expects us.

Lollio. I mistrust the madmen most; the fools will do
60 well enough; I have taken pains with them.

Alibius. Tush, they cannot miss; the more absurdity,
The more commends it, so no rough behaviours
Affright the ladies; they are nice things, thou know'st.

Lollio. You need not fear, sir; so long as we are there
65 with our commanding pizzles, they'll be as tame as the
ladies themselves.

45 *Why* ed. (We *Q*)
46 *fair understanding* don't distort my words
63 *nice* fastidious   65 *pizzles* whips

Alibius. I will see them once more rehearse before
    they go.

Lollio. I was about it, sir; look you to the madmen's
morris, and let me alone with the other; there is one or
two that I mistrust their fooling; I'll instruct them, and   70
then they shall rehearse the whole measure.

Alibius. Do so; I'll see the music prepar'd; but,
    Lollio,
By the way, how does my wife brook her restraint?
Does she not grudge at it?

Lollio. So, so; she takes some pleasure in the house,   75
she would abroad else; you must allow her a little more
length, she's kept too short.

Alibius. She shall along to Vermandero's with us;
That will serve her for a month's liberty.

Lollio. What's that on your face, sir?   80

Alibius. Where, Lollio? I see nothing.

Lollio. Cry you mercy, sir, 'tis your nose; it showed
    like the trunk of a young elephant.

Alibius. Away, rascal! I'll prepare the music, Lollio.
                             Exit ALIBIUS.

Lollio. Do, sir, and I'll dance the whilst. Tony, where   85
    art thou, Tony?

Enter ANTONIO.

Antonio. Here, cousin; where art thou?

Lollio. Come, Tony, the footmanship I taught you.

Antonio. I had rather ride, cousin.

Lollio. Ay, a whip take you; but I'll keep you out.   90
    Vault in; look you, Tony: fa, la, la, la, la.
                                 [Dances.]

Antonio. Fa, la, la, la, la.
                                 [Dances.]

Lollio. There, an honour.

82 *nose* cuckolding reference
93 *honour* bow

R—D

Antonio. Is this an honour, coz?

95   *Lollio.* Yes, and it please your worship.

Antonio. Does honour bend in the hams, coz?

Lollio. Marry, does it, as low as worship, squireship,
nay, yeomanry itself sometimes, from whence it first
stiffened; there, rise, a caper.

100   *Antonio.* Caper after an honour, coz?

Lollio. Very proper; for honour is but a caper, rises as
fast and high, has a knee or two, and falls to the ground
again. You can remember your figure, Tony?   *Exit.*

Antonio. Yes, cousin; when I see thy figure, I can
105   remember mine.

Enter ISABELLA, [*like a madwoman*].

Isabella. Hey, how he treads the air! Shough, shough,
     t'other way!

He burns his wings else; here's wax enough below,
Icarus, more than will be cancelled these eighteen moons;
He's down, he's down! What a terrible fall he had!
110   Stand up, thou son of Cretan Dedalus,
*   And let us tread the lower labyrinth;
I'll bring thee to the clue.

Antonio. Prithee, coz, let me alone.

Isabella. Art thou not drown'd?
115   About thy head I saw a heap of clouds,
Wrapp'd like a Turkish turban; on thy back
A crook'd chameleon-colour'd rainbow hung
Like a tiara down unto thy hams.

Let me suck out those billows in thy belly;
120   Hark how they roar and rumble in the straits!
Bless thee from the pirates.

Antonio. Pox upon you; let me alone!

101 *rises* ed. (rise *Q*)   103 *figure* (1) dance-step (2) face
106 *he* ed. (she *Q*)   108 *cancelled* used up (as sealing-wax on
    deeds)   120 *straits* ed. (streets *Q*)

Isabella. Why shouldst thou mount so high as Mer-
  cury,
Unless thou hadst reversion of his place?
Stay in the moon with me, Endymion,   125
And we will rule these wild, rebellious waves,
That would have drown'd my love.
    Antonio. I'll kick thee if again thou touch me,
Thou wild unshapen antic; I am no fool,
You bedlam!
    Isabella.   But you are, as sure as I am, mad.   130
Have I put on this habit of a frantic,
With love as full of fury, to beguile
The nimble eye of watchful jealousy,
And am I thus rewarded?

                              [*Reveals herself.*]
    Antonio.   Ha, dearest beauty!
    Isabella. No, I have no beauty now,   135
Nor never had, but what was in my garments.
You, a quick-sighted lover? Come not near me!
Keep your caparisons, y'are aptly clad;
I came a feigner to return stark mad.

                                                   Exit.

                    Enter LOLLIO.

    Antonio. Stay, or I shall change condition,   140
And become as you are.
    Lollio. Why, Tony, whither now? Why, fool?
    Antonio. Whose fool, usher of idiots? You coxcomb!
I have fool'd too much.
    Lollio. You were best be mad another while then.   145
    Antonio. So I am, stark mad; I have cause enough;
And I could throw the full effects on thee,
And beat thee like a fury.

124 *reversion of his place* hopes of succeeding him.

Lollio. Do not, do not; I shall not forbear the gentle-
150 man under the fool, if you do; alas, I saw through your
fox-skin before now! Come, I can give you comfort;
my mistress loves you, and there is as arrant a madman
i' th' house as you are a fool, your rival, whom she loves
not; if after the masque we can rid her of him, you earn
155 her love, she says, and the fool shall ride her.

Antonio. May I believe thee?

Lollio. Yes, or you may choose whether you will or no.

Antonio. She's eas'd of him; I have a good quarrel
on't.

160 *Lollio.* Well, keep your old station yet, and be quiet.

Antonio. Tell her I will deserve her love.

[*Exit.*]

Lollio. And you are like to have your desire.

Enter FRANCISCUS.

Franciscus (*sings*). 'Down, down, down a-down a-
down' and then with a horse-trick,
165 To kick Latona's forehead, and break her bowstring.

Lollio. This is t'other counterfeit; I'll put him out of
his humour. [*Takes out letter and reads.*] 'Sweet lady,
having now cast off this counterfeit cover of a madman, I appear to your best judgment a true and faithful
170 lover of your beauty.' This is pretty well for a madman.

Franciscus. Ha! What's that?

Lollio. 'Chide those perfections in you which have
made me imperfect.'

Franciscus. I am discovered to the fool.

175 *Lollio.* I hope to discover the fool in you, ere I have
done with you. 'Yours all, or one beside himself, Franciscus.' This madman will mend sure.

Franciscus. What do you read, sirrah?

151 *fox-skin* disguise   164 *horse-trick* horse-play, prank
165 *Latona* here Diana   168 *cast off* ed. (cast *Q*)
172 *which have* ed. (which *Q*)

Lollio. Your destiny, sir; you'll be hanged for this trick, and another that I know.   180

Franciscus. Art thou of counsel with thy mistress?

Lollio. Next her apron strings.

Franciscus. Give me thy hand.

Lollio. Stay, let me put yours in my pocket first [*puts away the letter*]; your hand is true, is it not? It will not 185 pick? I partly fear it, because I think it does lie.

Franciscus. Not in a syllable.

Lollio. So; if you love my mistress so well as you have handled the matter here, you are like to be cured of your madness.   190

Franciscus. And none but she can cure it.

Lollio. Well, I'll give you over then, and she shall cast your water next.

Franciscus. Take for thy pains past.[*Gives him money.*]

Lollio. I shall deserve more, sir, I hope; my mistress 195 loves you, but must have some proof of your love to her.

Franciscus. There I meet my wishes.

Lollio. That will not serve, you must meet her enemy and yours.

Franciscus. He's dead already!   200

Lollio. Will you tell me that, and I parted but now with him?

Franciscus. Show me the man.

Lollio. Ay, that's a right course now; see him before you kill him in any case, and yet it needs not go so far 205 neither; 'tis but a fool that haunts the house and my mistress in the shape of an idiot; bang but his fool's coat well-favouredly, and 'tis well.

Franciscus. Soundly, soundly!

Lollio. Only reserve him till the masque be past; and 210 if you find him not now in the dance yourself, I'll show you. In, in! My master!

186 *pick* steal   192–3 *cast your water* diagnose your ailment

Franciscus. He handles him like a feather. Hey!

[*Exit dancing.*]

Enter ALIBIUS.

Alibius. Well said; in a readiness, Lollio?

215   *Lollio.* Yes, sir.

Alibius. Away then, and guide them in, Lollio;
Entreat your mistress to see this sight.
Hark, is there not one incurable fool
That might be begg'd? I have friends.

220   *Lollio.* I have him for you, one that shall deserve
it too.   [*Exit.*]

Alibius. Good boy, Lollio.

[*Enter* ISABELLA, *then* LOLLIO *with* MADMEN *and* FOOLS.]

The MADMEN *and* FOOLS *dance.*

Alibius. 'Tis perfect; well, fit but once these strains,
We shall have coin and credit for our pains.

Exeunt.

Act V, Scene i

Enter BEATRICE. *A clock strikes one.*

Beatrice. One struck, and yet she lies by't!—Oh, my
fears!
This strumpet serves her own ends, 'tis apparent now,
Devours the pleasure with a greedy appetite,
And never minds my honour or my peace,

5   Makes havoc of my right; but she pays dearly for't:
No trusting of her life with such a secret,
That cannot rule her blood to keep her promise.
Beside, I have some suspicion of her faith to me,

214 *Well said* well done
219 *begg'd* sought as ward, to enjoy profits of his estate.

Because I was suspected of my lord,
And it must come from her. Hark! By my horrors,   10
Another clock strikes two!   *Strikes two.*

Enter DE FLORES.

De Flores.   Pist, where are you?
Beatrice. De Flores?
De Flores.   Ay; is she not come from him yet?
Beatrice. As I am a living soul, not.
De Flores.   Sure the devil
Hath sow'd his itch within her; who'd trust
A waiting-woman?
Beatrice.   I must trust somebody.   15
De Flores. Push! They are termagants;
Especially when they fall upon their masters,
And have their ladies' first-fruits; th' are mad whelps,
You cannot stave 'em off from game royal; then
You are so harsh and hardy, ask no counsel,   20
And I could have help'd you to an apothecary's daugh-
     ter,
Would have fall'n off before eleven, and thank'd you
     too.
Beatrice. O me, not yet? This whore forgets herself.
De Flores. The rascal fares so well; look, y'are undone,
The day-star, by this hand! See Phosphorus plain
     yonder.   25
Beatrice. Advise me now to fall upon some ruin,
There is no counsel safe else.
De Flores.   Peace, I ha't now;
For we must force a rising, there's no remedy.
Beatrice. How? Take heed of that.
De Flores. Tush, be you quiet, or else give over all.   30
Beatrice. Prithee, I ha' done then.

22 *thank'd* ed. (thank *Q*)
25 *Phosphorus* (Bosphorus *Q*) morning-star
26 *ruin* desperate measure

De Flores.   This is my reach: I'll set
Some part afire of Diaphanta's chamber.

 Beatrice. How? Fire, sir? That may endanger the
  whole house.

 De Flores. You talk of danger when your fame's on
  fire?

 Beatrice. That's true; do what thou wilt now.

35 *De Flores.*   Push! I aim
At a most rich success, strikes all dead sure;
The chimney being afire, and some light parcels
Of the least danger in her chamber only,
If Diaphanta should be met by chance then,

40 Far from her lodging—which is now suspicious—
It would be thought her fears and affrights then
Drove her to seek for succour; if not seen
Or met at all, as that's the likeliest,
For her own shame she'll hasten towards her lodging;

45 I will be ready with a piece high-charg'd,
As 'twere to cleanse the chimney; there 'tis proper now,
But she shall be the mark.

 Beatrice.   I'm forc'd to love thee now,
'Cause thou provid'st so carefully for my honour.

 De Flores. 'Slid, it concerns the safety of us both,
* Our pleasure and continuance.

50 *Beatrice.*   One word now, prithee;
How for the servants?

 De Flores. I'll despatch them
Some one way, some another in the hurry,
For buckets, hooks, ladders; fear not you;
The deed shall find its time; and I've thought since

55 Upon a safe conveyance for the body too.
How this fire purifies wit! Watch you your minute.

 Beatrice. Fear keeps my soul upon't, I cannot stray
  from't.

31 *reach* plan   45 *piece* fire-arm

Enter ALONZO'S *ghost.*

De Flores. Ha! What art thou that tak'st away the
    light
'Twixt that star and me? I dread thee not;
'Twas but a mist of conscience—All's clear again.   60
                              Exit.

Beatrice. Who's that, De Flores? Bless me! It slides
    by;
                          [*Exit ghost.*]
Some ill thing haunts the house; 't has left behind it
A shivering sweat upon me; I'm afraid now;
This night hath been so tedious. Oh, this strumpet!
Had she a thousand lives, he should not leave her   65
Till he had destroy'd the last.—List! Oh, my terrors!
Three struck by Saint Sebastian's!—
                         Struck three o'clock.

Within. Fire, fire, fire!
Beatrice. Already! How rare is that man's speed!
How heartily he serves me! His face loathes one,   70
But look upon his care, who would not love him?
The east is not more beauteous than his service.

Within. Fire, fire, fire!
    Enter DE FLORES; *servants pass over, ring a bell.*
De Flores. Away, despatch! Hooks, buckets, ladders!
    That's well said;
The fire-bell rings, the chimney works; my charge;   75
The piece is ready.
                           Exit.

Beatrice.   Here's a man worth loving—

    Enter DIAPHANTA.

Oh, y'are a jewel!
    Diaphanta.   Pardon frailty, madam;

75 *charge* powder

In troth I was so well, I ev'n forgot myself.

Beatrice. Y'have made trim work.

Diaphanta.   What?

Beatrice.   Hie quickly to your chamber;
Your reward follows you.

80   *Diaphanta.*   I never made
So sweet a bargain.   *Exit.*

Enter ALSEMERO.

Alsemero.   O my dear Joanna,
Alas, art thou risen too? I was coming,
My absolute treasure.

Beatrice.   When I miss'd you,
I could not choose but follow.

Alsemero.   Th'art all sweetness;
The fire is not so dangerous.

85   *Beatrice.*   Think you so, sir?

Alsemero. I prithee tremble not; believe me, 'tis not.

Enter VERMANDERO *and* JASPERINO.

Vermandero. Oh, bless my house and me!

Alsemero.   My lord your father.

Enter DE FLORES *with a piece.*

Vermandero. Knave, whither goes that piece?

De Flores.   To scour the chimney.
    Exit.

Vermandero. Oh, well said, well said;

90   That fellow's good on all occasions.

Beatrice. A wondrous necessary man, my lord.

Vermandero. He hath a ready wit, he's worth 'em all,
    sir;
Dog at a house of fire; I ha' seen him sing'd ere now.
    The piece goes off.

93 *Dog at* adept at

—Ha, there he goes.

Beatrice.   'Tis done.

Alsemero.   Come, sweet, to bed now;
Alas, thou wilt get cold.

Beatrice.   Alas, the fear keeps that out;   95
My heart will find no quiet till I hear
How Diaphanta, my poor woman, fares;
It is her chamber, sir, her lodging chamber.

Vermandero. How should the fire come there?

Beatrice. As good a soul as ever lady countenanc'd,   100
But in her chamber negligent and heavy;
She 'scap'd a mine twice.

Vermandero.   Twice?

Beatrice.   Strangely twice, sir.

Vermandero. Those sleepy sluts are dangerous in a
     house,
And they be ne'er so good.

Enter DE FLORES.

De Flores.   O poor virginity,
Thou hast paid dearly for't!

Vermandero.   Bless us! What's that?   105

De Flores. A thing you all knew once—Diaphanta's
     burnt.

Beatrice. My woman, oh, my woman!

De Flores.   Now the flames
Are greedy of her; burnt, burnt, burnt to death, sir!

Beatrice. Oh, my presaging soul!

Alsemero.   Not a tear more;
I charge you by the last embrace I gave you   110
In bed before this rais'd us.

Beatrice.   Now you tie me;
Were it my sister, now she gets no more.

Enter SERVANT.

102 *mine* catastrophe, danger

Vermandero. How now?

Servant. All danger's past; you may now take your
115   rests, my lords, the fire is throughly quench'd; ah,
poor gentlewoman, how soon was she stifled!

Beatrice. De Flores, what is left of her inter,
And we as mourners all will follow her;
I will entreat that honour to my servant,
Ev'n of my lord himself.

120   *Alsemero.*   Command it, sweetness.

Beatrice. Which of you spied the fire first?

De Flores.   'Twas I, madam.

Beatrice. And took such pains in't too? A double
     goodness!
'Twere well he were rewarded.

Vermandero.   He shall be;
De Flores, call upon me.

Alsemero.   And upon me, sir.

             Exeunt [all except DE FLORES.]

De Flores. Rewarded? Precious! Here's a trick be-
125   yond me;
I see in all bouts both of sport and wit,
Always a woman strives for the last hit.

                     Exit.

Act V, Scene ii

Enter TOMAZO.

Tomazo. I cannot taste the benefits of life
With the same relish I was wont to do.
Man I grow weary of, and hold his fellowship
A treacherous, bloody friendship; and because
5   I am ignorant in whom my wrath should settle,
I must think all men villains, and the next

I meet, whoe'er he be, the murderer
Of my most worthy brother.—Ha! What's he?

Enter DE FLORES, *passes over the stage.*

Oh, the fellow that some call honest De Flores;
But methinks honest was hard bested   10
To come there for a lodging, as if a queen
Should make her palace of a pest-house.
I find a contrariety in nature
Betwixt that face and me; the least occasion
Would give me game upon him; yet he's so foul   15
One would scarce touch him with a sword he loved
And made account of; so most deadly venemous,
He would go near to poison any weapon
That should draw blood on him; one must resolve
Never to use that sword again in fight,   20
In way of honest manhood, that strikes him;
Some river must devour't, 'twere not fit
That any man should find it.—What, again?

Enter DE FLORES.

He walks a' purpose by, sure, to choke me up,
To infect my blood.
    De Flores.   My worthy noble lord!   25
    Tomazo. Dost offer to come near and breathe upon
      me?   [*Strikes him.*]
    De Flores. A blow!   [*Draws his sword.*]
    Tomazo.   Yea, are you so prepar'd?
I'll rather, like a soldier, die by th' sword
                         [*Draws.*]
Than like a politician by thy poison.
    De Flores. Hold, my lord, as you are honourable.   30
    Tomazo. All slaves that kill by poison are still cowards.

---

15 *give me game* make me challenge him
16 *touch him* ed. (touch *Q*)

De Flores [*aside*]. I cannot strike; I see his brother's
     wounds
Fresh bleeding in his eye, as in a crystal.—
I will not question this; I know y'are noble;
35   I take my injury with thanks given, sir,
Like a wise lawyer; and as a favour
Will wear it for the worthy hand that gave it.—
[*aside*]. Why this from him that yesterday appear'd
So strangely loving to me?
40   Oh, but instinct is of a subtler strain;
Guilt must not walk so near his lodge again;
He came near me now.

                                  Exit.

Tomazo. All league with mankind I renounce for ever,
Till I find this murderer; not so much
45   As common courtesy, but I'll lock up;
For in the state of ignorance I live in,
A brother may salute his brother's murderer,
And wish good speed to th' villain in a greeting.

         Enter VERMANDERO, ALIBIUS, *and* ISABELLA.

Vermandero. Noble Piracquo!
Tomazo.   Pray keep on your way, sir,
I've nothing to say to you.
50   *Vermandero.*   Comforts bless you, sir.
Tomazo. I have forsworn compliment, in troth I have,
     sir;
As you are merely man, I have not left
A good wish for you, nor any here.
Vermandero. Unless you be so far in love with grief
55   You will not part from't upon any terms,
We bring that news will make a welcome for us.
Tomazo. What news can that be?
Vermandero.   Throw no scornful smile
Upon the zeal I bring you, 'tis worth more, sir.

Two of the chiefest men I kept about me
I hide not from the law or your just vengeance.   60
   Tomazo. Ha!
   Vermandero. To give your peace more ample satis-
      faction,
Thank these discoverers.
   Tomazo.   If you bring that calm,
Name but the manner I shall ask forgiveness in
For that contemptuous smile upon you: 65
I'll perfect it with reverence that belongs
Unto a sacred altar.   [*Kneels.*]
   Vermandero.   Good sir, rise;
Why, now you overdo as much a' this hand
As you fell short a' t'other. Speak, Alibius.
   Alibius. 'Twas my wife's fortune, as she is most lucky   70
At a discovery, to find out lately
Within our hospital of fools and madmen
Two counterfeits slipp'd into these disguises;
Their names, Franciscus and Antonio.
   Vermandero. Both mine, sir, and I ask no favour for
      'em.   75
   Alibius. Now that which draws suspicion to their
      habits,
The time of their disguisings agrees justly
With the day of the murder.
   Tomazo.   O blest revelation!
   Vermandero. Nay more, nay more, sir—I'll not spare
      mine own
In way of justice—they both feign'd a journey   80
To Briamata, and so wrought out their leaves;
My love was so abus'd in't.
   Tomazo.   Time's too precious
To run in waste now; you have brought a peace
The riches of five kingdoms could not purchase.
Be my most happy conduct; I thirst for 'em;   85

Like subtle lightning will I wind about 'em,
And melt their marrow in 'em.

Exeunt.

Act V, Scene iii

Enter ALSEMERO *and* JASPERINO.

Jasperino. Your confidence, I'm sure, is now of proof.
The prospect from the garden has show'd
Enough for deep suspicion.
    Alsemero.   The black mask
That so continually was worn upon't
5   Condemns the face for ugly ere't be seen;
Her despite to him, and so seeming bottomless.
    Jasperino. Touch it home then; 'tis not a shallow
        probe
Can search this ulcer soundly; I fear you'll find it
Full of corruption; 'tis fit I leave you,
10 She meets you opportunely from that walk;
She took the back door at his parting with her.
                     Exit JASPERINO
    Alsemero. Did my fate wait for this unhappy stroke
At my first sight of woman?—She's here.

Enter BEATRICE.

    Beatrice. Alsemero!
    Alsemero.   How do you?
    Beatrice.   How do I?
15 Alas! how do you? You look not well.
    Alsemero. You read me well enough, I am not well.
    Beatrice. Not well, sir? Is't in my power to better
        you?
    Alsemero. Yes.
    Beatrice.   Nay, then y'are cur'd again.

Alsemero. Pray resolve me one question, lady.

Beatrice.   If I can.

Alsemero. None can so sure. Are you honest?   20

Beatrice. Ha, ha, ha! That's a broad question, my
lord.

Alsemero. But that's not a modest answer, my lady.
Do you laugh? My doubts are strong upon me.

Beatrice. 'Tis innocence that smiles, and no rough
brow

Can take away the dimple in her cheek.   25
Say I should strain a tear to fill the vault,
Which would you give the better faith to?

Alsemero. 'Twere but hypocrisy of a sadder colour,
But the same stuff; neither your smiles nor tears
Shall move or flatter me from my belief: 30
You are a whore!

Beatrice.   What a horrid sound it hath!
It blasts a beauty to deformity;
Upon what face soever that breath falls,
It strikes it ugly; oh, you have ruin'd
What you can ne'er repair again.

Alsemero.   I'll all   35
Demolish, and seek out truth within you,
If there be any left; let your sweet tongue
Prevent your heart's rifling; there I'll ransack
And tear out my suspicion.

Beatrice.   You may, sir,
'Tis an easy passage; yet, if you please,   40
Show me the ground whereon you lost your love;
My spotless virtue may but tread on that
Before I perish.

Alsemero.   Unanswerable!
A ground you cannot stand on; you fall down
Beneath all grace and goodness when you set   45

26 *vault* sky

Your ticklish heel on't; there was a visor
O'er that cunning face, and that became you;
Now impudence in triumph rides upon't;
How comes this tender reconcilement else
'Twixt you and your despite, your rancorous loathing,
De Flores? He that your eye was sore at sight of,
He's now become your arm's supporter, your
Lip's saint!

    Beatrice. Is there the cause?

    Alsemero.   Worse; your lust's devil,
Your adultery!

    Beatrice.   Would any but yourself say that,
'Twould turn him to a villain.

    Alsemero.   'Twas witness'd
By the counsel of your bosom, Diaphanta.

    Beatrice. Is your witness dead then?

    Alsemero.   'Tis to be fear'd
It was the wages of her knowledge; poor soul,
She liv'd not long after the discovery.

    Beatrice. Then hear a story of not much less horror
Than this your false suspicion is beguil'd with;
To your bed's scandal I stand up innocence,
Which even the guilt of one black other deed
Will stand for proof of: your love has made me
A cruel murd'ress.

    Alsemero.   Ha!

    Beatrice   A bloody one;
I have kiss'd poison for't, strok'd a serpent:
That thing of hate, worthy in my esteem
Of no better employment, and him most worthy
To be so employ'd, I caus'd to murder
That innocent Piracquo, having no
Better means than that worst, to assure
Yourself to me.

    62 *stand up* oppose

Alsemero.   Oh, the place itself e'er since
Has crying been for vengeance, the temple
Where blood and beauty first unlawfully
Fir'd their devotion and quench'd the right one;   75
'Twas in my fears at first, 'twill have it now;
Oh, thou art all deform'd!
 Beatrice.   Forget not, sir,
It for your sake was done; shall greater dangers
Make the less welcome?
 Alsemero   Oh, thou shouldst have gone
A thousand leagues about to have avoided   80
This dangerous bridge of blood! Here we are lost.
 Beatrice. Remember I am true unto your bed.
 Alsemero. The bed itself's a charnel, the sheets shrouds
For murder'd carcasses. It must ask pause
What I must do in this; meantime you shall   85
Be my prisoner only. Enter my closet;   *Exit* BEATRICE
I'll be your keeper yet. Oh, in what part
Of this sad story shall I first begin?—Ha!
This same fellow has put me in.—

Enter DE FLORES.

        De Flores!
 De Flores. Noble Alsemero!
 Alsemero.   I can tell you   90
News, sir; my wife has her commended to you.
 De Flores. That's news indeed, my lord; I think she
  would
Commend me to the gallows if she could,
She ever lov'd me so well; I thank her.
 Alsemero. What's this blood upon your band, De
  Flores?   95

74 *blood* physical desire
75 *right one* religious devotion
76 *'twill . . . now* i.e. the temple will have its vengeance
89 *put me in* started me off   95 *band* collar

De Flores. Blood? No, sure, 'twas wash'd since.

Alsemero.   Since when, man?

De Flores. Since t'other day I got a knock
In a sword-and-dagger school; I think 'tis out.

Alsemero. Yes, 'tis almost out, but 'tis perceiv'd
    though.

100 I had forgot my message; this it is:
What price goes murder?

De Flores.   How sir?

Alsemero.   I ask you, sir;
My wife's behindhand with you, she tells me,
For a brave bloody blow you gave for her sake
Upon Piracquo.

De Flores.   Upon? 'Twas quite through him, sure;
Has she confess'd it?

105 *Alsemero.*   As sure as death to both of you,
And much more than that.

De Flores.   It could not be much more;
'Twas but one thing, and that—she's a whore.

Alsemero. It could not choose but follow; oh,
    cunning devils!
How should blind men know you from fair-fac'd saints?

110 *Beatrice, within.* He lies, the villain does belie me!

De Flores. Let me go to her, sir.

Alsemero.   Nay, you shall to her.
Peace, crying crocodile, your sounds are heard!
Take your prey to you, get you in to her, sir.

                              Exit DE FLORES.

I'll be your pander now; rehearse again

115 Your scene of lust, that you may be perfect
When you shall come to act it to the black audience
Where howls and gnashings shall be music to you.
Clip your adult'ress freely, 'tis the pilot

102 *behindhand with* beholding to   108 *It* ed. (I *Q*)

Will guide you to the Mare Mortuum,
Where you shall sink to fathoms bottomless.　　120

Enter VERMANDERO, ALIBIUS, ISABELLA, TOMAZO,
FRANCISCUS, *and* ANTONIO.

Vermandero. Oh, Alsemero. I have a wonder for you.

Alsemero. No, sir, 'tis I, I have a wonder for you.

Vermandero. I have suspicion near as proof itself
For Piracquo's murder.

Alsemero.　　　　　Sir, I have proof
Beyond suspicion for Piracquo's murder.　　125

Vermandero. Beseech you, hear me; these two have
　　been disguis'd
E'er since the deed was done.

Alsemero.　　　　　I have two other
That were more close disguis'd than your two could be
E'er since the deed was done.

Vermandero. You'll hear me—these mine own
　　servants—　　130

Alsemero. Hear me: those nearer than your servants,
That shall acquit them and prove them guiltless.

Franciscus. That may be done with easy truth, sir.

Tomazo. How is my cause bandied through your
　　delays!
'Tis urgent in my blood and calls for haste;　　135
Give me a brother alive or dead;
Alive, a wife with him; if dead, for both
A recompense for murder and adultery.

Beatrice, within. Oh, oh, oh!

Alsemero.　　　　　Hark! 'Tis coming to you.

De Flores, within. Nay, I'll along for company.

Beatrice, within　　　　　Oh, oh!　　140

Vermandero. What horrid sounds are these?

119 *Mare Mortuum* Dead Sea　　135 *my blood* ed. (blood *Q*)
138 *adultery* Beatrice's rejection of Alonzo for Alsemero

Alsemero. Come forth, you twins of mischief.

Enter DE FLORES, *bringing in* BEATRICE [*wounded*].

De Flores. Here we are; if you have any more
To say to us, speak quickly, I shall not
145 Give you the hearing else; I am so stout yet,
And so, I think, that broken rib of mankind.
    Vermandero. An host of enemies ent'red my citadel
Could not amaze like this: Joanna! Beatrice-Joanna!
    Beatrice. Oh, come not near me, sir, I shall defile
        you;
150 I am that of your blood was taken from you
For your better health; look no more upon't,
But cast it to the ground regardlessly,
Let the common sewer take it from distinction.
Beneath the stars, upon yon meteor
155 Ever hung my fate, 'mongst things corruptible;
I ne'er could pluck it from him; my loathing
Was prophet to the rest, but ne'er believ'd;
Mine honour fell with him, and now my life.
Alsemero, I am a stranger to your bed,
160 Your bed was cozen'd on the nuptial night,
For which your false bride died.
    Alsemero.   Diaphanta!
    De Flores. Yes, and the while I coupled with your
        mate
At barley-break; now we are left in hell.
    Vermandero. We are all there, it circumscribes us
        here.
165   *De Flores.* I lov'd this woman in spite of her heart;
Her love I earn'd out of Piracquo's murder.
    Tomazo. Ha! my brother's murderer?
    De Flores.   Yes, and her honour's prize

151 *better health* through blood-letting 153 *distinction* perception
154 *meteor* i.e. De Flores (corrupt body as opposed to a star)
155 *hung* ed. (hang *Q*)   164 *us here* ed. (here *Q*)

Was my reward; I thank life for nothing
But that pleasure; it was so sweet to me
That I have drunk up all, left none behind   170
For any man to pledge me.
 Vermandero.   Horrid villain!
Keep life in him for further tortures.
 De Flores.   No!
I can prevent you; here's my penknife still;
It is but one thread more, [*stabs himself*] and now 'tis
  cut.
Make haste, Joanna, by that token to thee,   175
Canst not forget, so lately put in mind;
I would not go to leave thee far behind.

              Dies

 Beatrice. Forgive me, Alsemero, all forgive;
'Tis time to die when 'tis a shame to live.   *Dies*
 Vermandero. Oh, my name is enter'd now in that
  record,   180
Where till this fatal hour 'twas never read.
 Alsemero. Let it be blotted out; let your heart lose it,
And it can never look you in the face,
Nor tell a tale behind the back of life
To your dishonour; justice hath so right   185
The guilty hit that innocence is quit
By proclamation, and may joy again.
Sir, you are sensible of what truth hath done;
'Tis the best comfort that your grief can find.
 Tomazo. Sir, I am satisfied; my injuries   190
Lie dead before me; I can exact no more,
Unless my soul were loose, and could o'ertake
Those black fugitives that are fled from thence,
To take a second vengeance; but there are wraths
Deeper than mine, 'tis to be fear'd, about 'em.   195
 Alsemero. What an opacous body had that moon
That last chang'd on us! Here's beauty chang'd

To ugly whoredom; here, servant obedience
To a master-sin, imperious murder;
200 I, a suppos'd husband, chang'd embraces
With wantonness, but that was paid before;
Your change is come too, from an ignorant wrath
To knowing friendship. Are there any more on's?
    Antonio. Yes, sir, I was changed too, from a little
205 ass as I was to a great fool as I am, and had like
to ha' been changed to the gallows, but that
you know my innocence always excuses me.
    Franciscus. I was chang'd from a little wit to be
        stark mad,
Almost for the same purpose.
    Isabella.   Your change is still behind
210 But deserve best your transformation:
You are a jealous coxcomb, keep schools of folly,
And teach your scholars how to break your own head.
    Alibius. I see all apparent, wife, and will change now
Into a better husband, and never keep
215 Scholars that shall be wiser than myself.
    Alsemero. Sir, you have yet a son's duty living,
Please you accept it; let that your sorrow,
As it goes from your eye, go from your heart;
Man and his sorrow at the grave must part.

201 *paid before* by Diaphanta's death

EPILOGUE

220   *Alsemero.* All we can do to comfort one another,
       To stay a brother's sorrow for a brother,
       To dry a child from the kind father's eyes,
       Is to no purpose, it rather multiplies;
       Your only smiles have power to cause relive
225   The dead again, or in their rooms to give
       Brother a new brother, father a child;
       If these appear, all griefs are reconcil'd.   *Exeunt omnes*

FINIS

CRITICAL NOTES

5   I.i, 1. *temple*. The misuse of the church for wooing is made much of by Reynolds: 'It is both a griefe and a scandall to any true Christian's heart that the church ordained for thanks-giving and Prayer unto God, should be made a Stewes, or at least, a place for men to meet and court Ladies.'

    This moral note is struck by Rowley all through scene i in his religious imagery (e.g. lines 8, 34, 155) and is referred to specifically in Act V, scene iii (lines 72-6).

8   I.i, 91. *board her*. A very usual nautical metaphor, used more than once by Reynolds to describe Alsemero's advances to Beatrice-Joanna in the temple.

9   I.i, 117. *sound*. Q, Bawcutt; *found*, all other eds. Bawcutt's return to Q reading seems justifiable—'the possession of a slight imperfection is a criterion of normality.' (i.e. soundness).

9   I.i, 128. *cherry*. Alsemero may, indeed, as Barker suggests, have 'an allergy to cherries'; on the other hand, he may simply be using 'cherry' to imply something trifling.

10   I.i, 151. *cuckoo* (*what you call't*). Sexual innuendo. Bawcutt quotes Rowley's description, in *All's Lost by Lust*, III, iii, 103-8 of cuckoo pintle-roots as 'long upright things that grow a yard above the ground'.

11   I.i, 175. *Iulan*. Sampson suggests a reference to Iulus Ascanius, *Aeneid* (I,267).

15   ff. I.ii, Full of sexual allusions, e.g. (24–31) cuckold's horns and ring double entendre; (185) push-pin, child's game but also sexual implication.

20   I.ii, 203–6. *we three*. 'Antonio probably alludes to the old sign of *two* idiots' heads with an inscription,

           We three,

           Loggerheads be.' [*Dilke*] The spectator completes the trio.

24   II.i, 58. *standing toad-pool*. Offensive reference to De Flores' complexion. The image is not of the warty skin of the toad but of the toad-pool, the breeding place of corruption.

29   II.ii, 43. *the ugliest creature*. Doctrine much referred to by early seventeenth-century writers that everything in Nature is of some use: cf. Montaigne, *Essais* Book III, Ch. 1; Browne, *Rel. Med.* Bk. 1, § 16. 'I cannot tell by what Logick we call a Toad, a Bear, or an Elephant ugly; they being created in those outward shapes and forms which best express the action of their inward forms. . . .'

31   II.ii, 74. *prun'd*. 'A hawk is said to prune itself when it sets its feathers in order with its beak.' (*Bullen*.)

34   II.ii, 146. *blood*. Throughout the play the three meanings of blood: (i) life-blood, (ii) sensual desire, (iii) rank and birth, are constantly played upon.

34   II.ii, 162. *Push* Bawcutt (Puh *Q*) 'Push', as an ejaculation, is one of Middleton's trade-marks.

37   III.iii, 5. *Whistle . . . pipe after*. Bawcutt suggests a variant on the common tag 'to dance after someone's pipe.' But the familiar image of a bird in a cage responding to a whistle is more in keeping with Isabella's prisoner state. (Cf. Webster's very frequent

use of caged-bird imagery in both *The White Devil*
and *The Duchess of Malfi*.)

38   III.iii, 45. *spider*. Traditionally poisonous, cf. (among
many such refs.) Donne, *Twicknam Garden*.

'The spider love which transubstantiates all
And can convert Manna to gall.'

39   III.iii, 74. *seq*. The conversation between Lollio and
Franciscus is full of sexual overtones (e.g. lines 79, 84,
85) culminating in 'Give me leave to lie with thee.'

40   III.iii, 89. *lycanthropi*. Most memorable victim of ly-
canthropia (a madness in which the sufferer imagines
himself a wolf) was Ferdinand in Webster's *The
Duchess of Malfi*, V, ii (8 *seq*.)

43   III.iii, 172. *Last couple in hell*. An allusion to the game
of barley-brake—a game in which the men and women
coupled and one couple, stationed in a central area
called 'hell', attempted to catch the others as they
ran through. Obviously, from Sidney's long description (over 200 lines) of it, in an eclogue in the
1593 Folio, it was a mating-game, in which desires
ran high.

'So caught, him seem'd he caught of joyes the bell,
And thought it heaven so to be drawn to hell.
To hell he goes and *Nous* with him must dwell.'

cf. De Flores' reference, V, iii, 163.

['Barley' is often used as a truce term by children
at play in East Scotland, the Borders and many
parts of England.]

47   III.iii, 287. *lawyer's haven*. The port of riches towards
which all lawyers steer their course. While this disenchanted attitude to the law is prevalent in Jacobean
drama, Middleton had particular reason to be sen-
sitive about litigation involved, as he was, from the
age of 17, in his mother's endless law-suits. The law

plays a large part in his comedies (e.g. *Michaelmas Term, The Old Law, The Phoenix*).

47   III.iv, 9. *largely.* Dyce's alteration of *Q* reading to *largely commended* seems unnecessary.

48   III.iv, 18. *banquet . . . deed.* While it is true, as Bawcutt points out, that the *Q* reading makes sense, the phrase, 'my thoughts are at a banquet', if isolated by a semicolon or exclamation mark, conveys more of De Flores' gloating anticipation of his reward. The phrase may well carry the implication of sexual satisfaction, as Brooke suggests in *Bussy D'Ambois*, III, ii (194) (Revels edn.):

'I saw D'Ambois and she set close at a banquet.'

53   III.iv, 143–4. *chang'd.* i.e. transformed by death. The punning upon the title of the play, which seems a curious intrusion into the tragic action, is not restricted to the scenes attributed to Rowley. Here we have a foretaste of the play on 'chang'd' which ends Act V (iii, 196–214).

54   III.iv, 170. *turtle.* Cf. the unwitting irony of Beatrice's earlier condescending praise of De Flores 'pruning' himself like a hawk.

55   IV.i, 25. *Secrets in Nature.* Mizaldus, the French scholar and pseudo-scientist, has, according to Sampson, similar virginity tests to those in his writings, although probably Middleton is the author of these particular experiments. There is a somewhat comic virginity test in Middleton's earlier play, *The Mayor of Queenborough*, II, iii, where the test for a virgin is her ability to cure, by her touch, an epileptic fit—Horsus lies on the floor and blackmails his unchaste mistress, Roxana, by refusing to respond to her touch:

page

> *Horsus.* All this art shall not make me feel my legs.
> *Roxana.* I prithee, do not wilfully confound me.
> *Horsus.* Well, I'm content for this time to recover
>   To save thy credit, and bite in my pain;
>   But if thou ever fail'st me I will fall,
>   And thou shalt never get me up again.

The conspiracy which ensues between Roxana and Horsus to allow Roxana to marry the king, yet still remain Horsus's mistress, clearly points forward to the Beatrice–De Flores alliance.

56 IV.i, 59. *seq.* Diaphanta has to fill the dual rôle of honest virgin and bawdy waiting-maid. Her speeches are full of sexual meanings (e.g. lines 61, 63, 123) which give point to Beatrice's own double entendre,

> 'Y'are too quick, I fear, to be a maid.'

62 IV.ii, 51. *round-pack'd.* Most eds. gloss 'plump', though Schelling's suggestion of 'thoroughly dishonest' seems nearer Middleton's intention. Probably Middleton has both meanings in mind—firm curves, solid with sin—sins very much of the flesh, in fact. J. R. Mulryne has suggested to me 'a fleshly sinner', which covers both implications.

65 IV.ii, 128. *dove.* The last comparison of Beatrice to a dove was De Flores', as he held her captive in his arms, III, iii, 170. It is ironical that Alsemero and De Flores should be equally misled by her appearance.

67 IV.iii, 7 *seq.* Editors have differed considerably as to whether Isabella or Lollio reads the super-scription of the letter and at which point Isabella hands the letter to Lollio and takes it back from him. *Q* clearly attributes the whole speech 'The out's mad ...

madness' to Lollio. There seems to be a case for not inserting any such stage-directions as 'Gives him the letter.' (Bawcutt) or 'Reads' (Neilson). Lollio has delivered the letter to Isabella, has been much amused by the address and has an extremely good memory. (He has already quoted at length to taunt Isabella, III, iii, 234 *seq*.) He may well be quoting again here—'I had a taste on't', implying 'I noted it well.'

67   IV.iii, 9. *Knight of the Sun*. The references are to a popular Spanish romance, *The Mirror of Knighthood*, by Diego Ortunez de Calaborra, published in nine parts (1578–1601). The main significance of both address and letter seems to be the sexual innuendoes they contain, e.g. *chambermaid*, *Scorpio* (sign governing privy parts of body), *the middle region, the bellows-mender of Aeolus* (cf. *The Family of Love*, IV, i, for reference to bellows-makers and bawds), *grow and wither*, etc.

70   IV.iii, 111. *labyrinth*. Franciscus' reference to Isabella (line 8) implied that Alibius was a dragon; here Isabella's image is of the Minotaur. The metaphors used by Isabella to Antonio more than once echo Franciscus' speeches (cf. IV, iii (119–120) and line 10, 'the bellows-mender of Aeolus', cf. also 125 ff. and III, iii, 84 ff.). This would suggest some unintentional confusion between the two fools, if the general impression of the scene were not already one of confusion and madness.

76   V.i, 50. *continuance*. With one significant word Middleton gives the audience the feeling of a securely-established illicit relationship between De Flores and Beatrice. Here we have the familiar double-time technique; less than ten days have, in fact, elapsed

between the murder of Piracquo and the wedding of
Beatrice [IV, ii (7)]. Cf. the comment of T. S. Eliot.
'In the end, Beatrice having been *so long* [my italics]
the enforced conspirator of De Flores . . .'

NOTE ON THE TEXT

ALTHOUGH *The Changeling* was first licensed to be
acted in 1622, it was not printed for thirty years. The
text of the present edition is based on the British
Museum copy of the 1653 quarto. (Other copies are
in the Huntington Library and the Bodleian Library.)
The quarto text has been carefully collated with
recent editions of *The Changeling* and with that of
Bullen (1885) who, like Ellis (1887) and all succeeding
editors, was greatly indebted to the earlier editions of
Dilke (1815) and Dyce (1840). There are few difficulties
in the quarto but these early nineteenth-century editors
are largely responsible for considerable relineation and
insertion of asides and stage-directions. The punctuation in this text, as in most modern editions, changes
or adds to the quarto punctuation only where it seems
necessary in order to bring out the meaning of a
passage.
The Changeling has been printed many times in
this century, notably in the large anthologies of such
editors as Neilson, Sampson, Oliphant, Schelling,
and Hazelton Spencer. The fullest, most scholarly,
single edition of the play is that in the Revels series,
editor N. W. Bawcutt (1958).

*Printed in Great Britain by Cox and Wyman Ltd., London, Reading,
and Fakenham*